MANAGING GENDER

SUNY Series on Sport, Culture, and Social Relations
Cheryl L. Cole and Michael A. Messner, editors

MANAGING GENDER

*Affirmative Action and
Organizational Power in
Australian, Canadian,
and New Zealand Sport*

Jim McKay

State University of New York Press

Published by
State University of New York Press, Albany

© 1997 State University of New York

For information, address State University of New York Press, State University Plaza, Albany, N.Y., 12246

Production by Marilyn P. Semerad
Marketing by Bernadette LaManna

Library of Congress Cataloging-in-Publication Data

McKay, Jim, 1949–
    Managing gender : affirmative action and organizational power in Australian, Canadian, and New Zealand sport / Jim McKay.
        p.   cm. — (SUNY series on sport, culture, and social relations)
    Includes bibliographical references (p.   ) and index.
    ISBN 0-7914-3421-4 (hc : alk. paper). — ISBN 0-7914-3422-2 (pb : alk. paper)
    1. Sports for women—Social aspects—Australia. 2. Sports for women—Social aspects—Canada. 3. Sports for women—Social aspects--New Zealand. 4. Sex discrimination in sports—Australia. 5. Sex discrimination in sports—Canada. 6. Sex discrimination in sports--New Zealand. 7. Affirmative action programs—Australia.
8. Affirmative action programs—Canada. 9. Affirmative education programs—New Zealand. I. Title. II. Series.
GV709.18.A8M35 1997
353.53'082—dc21   96-53415
                                                                    CIP

10 9 8 7 6 5 4 3 2 1

To My Father

Contents

List of Tables   xi

Preface   xiii

Acknowledgments   xvii

List of Abbreviations   xxi

1. Introduction   1
   "The Search for Mr. Right"   1
   Profeminist Research   3
   Profeminist Research and Sport   7
   Summary   9

2. Theoretical Framework   13
   Thinking Institutionally about
     Gender and Organizations   13
   Gender and Social Constructionism   14
   Gendered Structures of Labor, Power,
     and Cathexis   14
   Implications for Gender and Sport   19
   Summary   23

3. The Corporate-Managerial State,
   Gender, and Sport   25
   The Rise of the Corporate-Managerial State   25

CONTENTS

Affirmative Action in
   The Corporate-Managerial State   26
Implications for Affirmative Action in Sport   30
Summary   44

4. Structures of Labor, Power, and Cathexis   47
   Methods   47
   Structures of Labor   51
   Structures of Power   70
   Structures of Cathexis   89
   Summary   94

5. "Doing" Affirmative Action   97
   Affirmative Action Opponents   97
   Affirmative Action Skeptics and Cynics   99
   Affirmative Action Advocates   101
   Organizations that Make Affirmative
      Action Work   113
   Summary   114

6. The Write Stuff? Media Representations of
   Affirmative Action in Australian Sport   117
   The Mass Media and the Social
      Construction of Gender   117
   Sports Journalism and "Groupthink"   119
   The "Paranoia of the Powerful"   125
   Summary   126

7. Hegemonic Masculinity and the Gender Politics of
   Affirmative Action Policy Research   129
   Intellectual Work and Cultural Policy   129
   Background to the Report   129
   The Commission's Response to the Report   132
   "Talking to the ISAs" Or "Dialogue with
      the Deaf"   138
   Summary   140

Contents

8. One Cheer for Affirmative Action 143
    The Limits of Affirmative Action 144
    Changing Organizational Cultures 145
    Changing Men 146
    Changing Sport 148
    Who and What Is Changing Whom? 154
    Summary 157

Appendix 1: Organizational Affiliations of
              Interviewees 159

Appendix 2: Questionnaire on the Status of Women
              Sport Executives 163

Appendix 3: Quantitative Summaries of Australian
              Respondents' Perceptions of Their
              Organizations 179

Bibliography 183

Subject Index 209

Name Index 213

List of Tables

Table 2.1 Ideal-type Representation of Connell's
Structures of Labor, Power, and Cathexis at
the Macro Level   20

Table 2.2 Percent of Women Executive Directors of
NSOs in Australia, Canada, and
New Zealand   22

Table 2.3 Ideal-type Representation of Gender
Structure of Core and Peripheral
Management Areas in Sporting
Organizations   22

Table 2.4 General Examples of Structures of Labor,
Power, and Cathexis in the Gender Regime
of Sport   23

Table 3.1 Ideal-type Comparison of Discourses in
Patriarchal-Welfare and Corporate-
Managerial State Formations in
Liberal-Democracies   29

Table 3.2 Ideal-type Subdiscourses of Affirmative
Action in Australian Sport   40

Table 3.3 Institutionally Specific Design Archetypes
for NSOs   45

LIST OF TABLES

Table 4.1 Structures of Hiring and Promotion By
Gatekeepers in Traditionally Male
Organizations   65

Table 4.2 Strategies Men and Women Use to "Manage"
Gender Relations in Organizations   74

Table 8.1 Changing Men through Changing Sports:
An 11-point Strategy   149

Table 8.2 Recommendations and Checklists on Sexual
Harassment for Coaches and Athletes   151

Table A.1 Australian Respondents' Perceptions of Why
Women Were Underrepresented in
Executive Positions   179

Table A.2 Australian Respondents' Perceptions of
Various Gender Structures and Processes in
Their Organizations   180

Table A.3 Australian Respondents' Perceptions of the
Role of a Women's Committee or Similar
Structure in Their Organizations   182

Preface

THIS BOOK EMANATED from an uneasiness I felt about an earlier one I wrote entitled, *No Pain, No Gain? Sport and Australian Culture*, in which I used a neo-Gramscian perspective to analyze inequalities of social class, race, and gender in Australian sport. Although I was convinced then—and still am—that a Gramscian position is fundamental for understanding some aspects of social inequalities in sport, I concluded that it could not explain gender inequalities satisfactorily. This was particularly evident in my investigation of state policies regarding sport. Although my study had been what Messner (1990a) terms "gender-conscious," it had not been "profeminist" and, therefore, lacked the insights necessary to illuminate just how pervasively sport is both constructed by and constructs gendered relations of power.

In order to obtain a more nuanced understanding of gender, sport, and state policies, I conducted approximately 100 in-depth interviews with managers of a variety of sporting organizations across Australia. My main goal was to analyze how these managers were implementing affirmative action programs for women in sport organizations run by state and federal governments. As will be discussed in chapter 7, this turned out to be a controversial project, as some members of the Australian Sports Commission, which funded the investigation, attempted to discredit my findings. This outcome motivated me to compare the Australian context with countries that also had affirmative action programs for women in sport.

Canada and New Zealand were obvious choices because the Canadian state's sport system, established in the 1960s, was a model for the Australian approach to national sports planning in the 1970s, while New Zealand drew on both of these countries' schemes when it created its national sports program in the 1980s. Moreover, the national agencies responsible for sport in each country—the Australian Sports Commission, Sport Canada, and the Hillary Commission for Recreation and Sport—have promoted themselves as "leading edge" organizations with respect to their affirmative action programs for women. Because I reside in Australia, I had neither the time nor the resources to complete in-depth interviews with a large sample of managers from a broad array of sporting organizations across Canada and New Zealand. Therefore, I decided to conduct in-depth interviews with most of the middle and senior managers in both Sport Canada and the Hillary Commission, as well as managers and members of the Canadian Association for the Advancement of Women and Sport, an influential "arm's length" advocacy group in the Canadian state.

My investigation showed that current affirmative action initiatives based on the premise of "getting more women into sport" have either been marginalized, trivialized, or incorporated into the androcentric cultures that pervade sporting organizations, the media, and the state. When affirmative action does get on the corporate-managerial agenda in the state sector, it tends either to receive rhetorical attention or to be couched in terms of what it can do to improve efficiency, rather than as a substantive commitment to social justice. I conclude that unless current affirmative action policies are directed at changing both men and the androcentric culture that is deeply embedded in the gender regimes of sporting organizations, they are unlikely to attract and retain more women managers.

In the first chapter I indicate the relevance of profeminist research to sport. In chapter 2 I sketch the main components of the social constructionist perspective that I used in the study. In chapter 3 I adopt a relatively abstract and macrolevel perspective to describe how state-initiated affirmative action policies in Australia, Canada, and New Zealand have been shaped by both androcentric and corporate-managerial regimes. Chapter 4 is a concrete and microlevel analysis of gendered structures of labor, power, and cathexis in sporting organizations. I argue that women's underrepresentation in managerial positions in these organizations is due to institutional barriers that systematically favor men and disadvantage women. A key factor in this respect is that chief components of work cultures are determined by and for married men with wives who stay at home, raise children, and do unpaid domestic labor. Chapter 5 specifically focuses on men and women managers' attitudes toward affirmative action. Chapter 6 examines how male journalists ridiculed affirmative action initiatives in Australian sport. Chapter 7 discusses the gender politics of doing research on affirmative action in sport. The final chapter discusses the limits and possibilities of affirmative action policies for changing relations of power between men and women in sporting organizations.

Acknowledgments

I AM GRATEFUL to The University of Queensland, the Australian Sports Commission, and the Canadian Studies Program for small grants that enabled me to collect some of the data. Julie Draper, formerly of the Australian Sports Commission, Marion Lay, formerly of Sport Canada, and Kereyn Smith of the Hillary Commission, made my investigation much easier by being generous hosts and introducing me to interviewees in their respective organizations.

I am indebted to Rhonda Bushby, Annette Corrigan, Libby Darlison, Geoff Lawrence, and Shona Thompson, who made constructive criticisms of various chapters; to Ann Hall, Helen Lenskyj, and an anonymous reviewer who made valuable suggestions on the entire manuscript; to Clay Morgan and Marilyn Semerad for their judicious editorial advice; and to Sean Cummings for a fine copyediting job.

Many thanks to Mike Messner for encouraging me to undertake the project and for increasing our field goal percentages by leaving the rim nice and loose for our all-too-infrequent sessions of hoops in his backyard.

As always, Jenny Figueiredo did a superb job in formatting the final draft.

Finally, I would like to extend my appreciation to the extremely overworked men and women in Australia, Canada, and New Zealand who took the time from their onerous schedules to talk to me.

In writing this book I have updated and extended some of my earlier research and integrated this with new work, and would like to thank the following publishers for permission to use sections from previously published material: Sage Publications for permission to reprint Tables 1 and 2 from M. Boyle and J. McKay "'You Leave Your Troubles at the Gate': A Case Study of the Exploitation of Older Women's Labor and 'Leisure.'" *Gender & Society* 9 (1995): 559, 573. Copyright © 1995 by Sage Publications, Inc. This appears as Table 2.4 in this book.

Macmillan Education Australia Pty Ltd for permission to use material from J. McKay, "Sport and the Social Construction of Gender," in *Society and Gender: An Introduction to Sociology*, edited by G. Lupton, T. Short, and R. Whip (Melbourne: Macmillan Education Australia Pty Ltd, 1992), 258–60.

Australian Journal of Political Science for permission to use material from J. McKay, "Masculine Hegemony, the State and the Incorporation of Gender Equity Discourse: The Case of Australian Sport," *Australian Journal of Political Science* 29(2) (1994), 82–95.

Culture and Policy for permission to use material from J. McKay, "Hegemonic Masculinity, the State and the Politics of Gender Equity Policy Research," *Culture and Policy* 5 (1994): 223–40.

In addition, I am grateful to the following publishers and/or authors for permission to reprint material from their publications:

Gareth Morgan, *Images of Organization* (New York: Sage Publications, 1986), Exhibit 6.5, 182–83, copyright © 1986 by Sage Publications. Reprinted by permission of Sage Publications, Inc. This appears as Table 4.2 in this book.

Lisa Kikulius, Trevor Slack, and Bob Hinings, "Institutionally Specific Design Archetypes: A Framework for Understanding Change in National Sport Organizations," *International Review for the Sociology of Sport* 27 (1992): 355, adaptation of Table 1. Used by permission of R. Oldenbourg Verlag GmbH. This appears as Table 2.2 in this book.

Jan Cameron for permission to use Table 5 on p. 66 of her book *Women Who Manage: Study of Volunteer National Sports Administrators* (Christchurch: Sociology Department, University of Canterbury, 1994). Copyright © 1994 by Jan Cameron. This appears as Table 2.2 in this book.

Barbara Reskin and Patricia Roos, *Job Queues, Gender Queues* (Philadelphia: Temple University Press, 1990), Figure 2.2 on page 33. Copyright © 1990 by Temple University Press. Reprinted by permission of Temple University Press. This appears as Table 4.1 in this book.

The Coaching Association of Canada, for permission to reprint from Helen Lenskyj, "Sexual Harassment: Female Athletes' Experiences and Coaches' Responsibilities." *Sports* 12: 6 (1992), 4–6. Copyright © 1992 by the Coaching Association of Canada. All Rights Reserved.

Michael Messner and Don Sabo, "Changing Men through Changing Sports," in *Sex, Violence and Power in Sports: Rethinking Masculinity*. Used by permission of The Crossing Press.

List of Abbreviations

ASC	Australian Sports Commission
ASRP	Applied Sports Research Program
CAAWS	Canadian Association for the Advancement of Women and Sport
HC	Hillary Commission for Recreation and Sport
HRSCLCA	House of Representatives Standing Committee on Legal and Constitutional Affairs
IOC	International Olympic Committee
NSO	National Sporting Organization
SC	Sport Canada

One

Introduction

At 4 A.M. ON THURSDAY, September 24, 1993, millions of television viewers in Australia were watching tens of thousands of people who had gathered around a giant electronic screen adjacent to Sydney's world-famous Opera House. Most of these people were hoping that the impending telecast from Monaco would reveal that Sydney had obtained one of sport's most glittering prizes—the right to host the Olympic Games in 2000. The crowd fell silent when Juan Antonio Samaranch, a former minister of sport in Francisco Franco's fascist regime in Spain and president of the International Olympic Committee (IOC), one of the most androcentric organizations in the world, appeared on screen to divulge the winner. The atmosphere was tense while Samaranch opened the envelope and waited for what seemed to the observers like an eternity before declaring the winner. When he announced that Sydney had triumphed, Australians began patriotic celebrations that had not been seen since almost 10 years to the day, when in another historic sporting event, Australia became the first challenger to defeat the United States in the America's Cup. In a portentously gendered statement, the then prime minister, Paul Keating, proclaimed that the outcome had put Australia "in the swim with the big boys."

There was immediate speculation about who the predominantly male members of the state government, the Australian Olympic Council, and the city council would select as the CEO and members of the organizing committee for the

1

Games. In her "Corporate Woman" column for *The Australian Financial Review* (Australia's equivalent of *The Wall Street Journal*), Sheryle Bagwell provided a short list of eminently qualified women whom she thought should be considered for CEO. Citing the contributions that women had made to the success of the tender, Bagwell (1993, p.17) opined that:

> . . . I thought the Olympic movement was about fairness and equity. After all, what better place than the sporting field to underline the truism that the winner is always the person on the day, whatever the gender? I admit that there is not much of a tradition of women running Olympic Games around the world. But wouldn't it be a great symbol for the Olympics that will herald in a change of millennium to have a women at the helm?

However, she was pessimistic that a woman actually would be chosen. As she noted, a Sydney newspaper had already set the gender agenda for the headhunters by dubbing the quest "The Search for Mr Right." But Bagwell was optimistic that the selectors would at least include some women members on the organizing committee. Her idealism was dashed when the composition of the committee was announced a few weeks later. Just one of the fourteen members was a woman, who was only added at the last minute after the embarrassed selectors realized that they initially had chosen only men. This belated decision to include a token woman evoked a barrage of criticism: a headline in *The Australian* proclaimed, "Women Cheated by Games Team Choice"; a letter to the editor of *The Sydney Morning Herald* was captioned, "Insult To All Women"; the head of the Women's Electoral Lobby said that the board was "a boring collection of Anglo-Saxon males."[1]

Putting thirteen men and one woman on the organizing committee for the 2000 Olympics is a graphic example of what Schein (1994) terms the "think male, think manager" mentality that pervades most organizations. But as I will attempt to demonstrate in this book, it is just one of myriad ways in which managerial practices are undergirded by male-centered assumptions. In order to study this androcentric culture of management, I maintain that it is necessary to use the perspectives of profeminism and social constructionism.

PROFEMINIST RESEARCH

Heterosexual men have responded to critiques of their relatively privileged position in society by women and gay men in several ways. Some have formed militant men's rights movements in order to counter perceived threats to their privileges. Others have blamed women for producing "soft" men and turned to mythopoetic activities like warrior weekends as a way of restoring "deep masculinity." A much smaller group has responded by taking on board some of the criticisms and embracing a profeminist, gay-affirmative and male-positive stance. Groups such as Men Against Sexual Assault, the National Organization of Men Against Sexism, and the White Ribbon campaign, which attempt to mobilize men to oppose other men's homophobic, misogynist, and violent behavior, are grass roots examples of this response. At the academic level, some men who are sympathetic to gay and feminist critiques have responded by basing their research on profeminist, gay-positive and male-positive principles (Brittan 1989; Brod and Kimmel 1994; Connell 1995; Kimmel and Messner 1995). From the perspective of profeminism, masculinity per se is not the problem, but rather the fact that a very restrictive way of being a man is idealized as *the* way that *all* men should act. For instance, Connell (1983, 22) correctly argues that masculinity is not, as some critics would have it, an impoverished phenomenon but a "plenitude." However, he goes on to state that "the specific richness of hegemonic masculinity is oppressive, being founded on, and enforcing, the subordination of women" (Connell 1983, 22). We can add the oppression of gay men to this observation.

3

A key feature of profeminist research is a commitment to "studying up" the gender order (Connell 1990c, 1992; Messner 1996). Consider the following statistics: in the United States a woman is raped every six minutes, and as many as one in four women may be raped during their lives; 1400 women are murdered by men every year; and a man beats a woman about every 15 seconds. A 1995 United Nations Development Program report on the global status of women revealed that:

- women constituted 70 percent of the 1.3 billion people living below the poverty line
- 75 percent of women workers were employed in low-paying and insecure jobs
- women made up 14 percent of administrators and managers and held just 10 percent of seats and 6 percent of ministerial positions in parliaments
- women earned 30 percent to 40 percent less than men
- between 15 percent and 20 percent of women in industrial countries reported that they had experienced frequent and serious sexual harassment, compelling 6 percent to 8 percent of them to quit their jobs
- 300 million women did not have the means to plan their pregnancies
- 500,000 and 100,000 died each year from childbirth problems and illegal abortions, respectively
- and two million were sexually mutilated annually.

The document recommended that in order to improve the status of women, governments should take affirmative action in legal, work, health, and educational spheres and strive to have 50 percent of the seats on public sector boards held by women by the year 2000. The report estimated that it would take an extra $20 billion a year to achieve this goal (*The Australian* 1995). Two recent studies by the International Labour Organization estimated that based on current trends, it will take women about 500 years to gain the same access as men to management positions and around 1,000 years for them to get equal representation in the upper echelons of political and economic power (*The Sydney Morning Herald* 1993; *The Weekend Australian* 1995).

In light of these facts, I believe that men should use their relatively privileged positions to study and promote gender justice. As I will demonstrate in chapter 7, this position is fraught with tensions. For instance, terms such as "profeminist men" or "male feminism" would appear to be an oxymoron (Heath 1986; Messner 1990a). As Connell (1987, 286) states, "In a gender order where men are advantaged and women are disadvantaged, major structural reform is, on the face of it, against men's interests." It is not surprising then, that profeminist men usually encounter hostility from antifeminist men and women and suspicion from some feminists (Duelli Klein 1983; Richardson and Robinson 1994). For some feminists, "men in feminism" evokes the question of "Now what are they up to?" (Bradshaw 1982) or charges of "cloak-and-dagger chauvinism" (Hester 1984). As Wise and Stanley (1984, 2) put it: "Men have been the subject of nearly all research to date, which has constituted 'men's studies,' so why should feminists add to this?" Bristow (1988, 121) also has noted the difficulty of men studying men by using feminist-inspired principles:

> In feminist theory . . . definitions of masculinity have made a point of noting that the one thing men are not equipped well to do is understanding just what they *are* as men, especially when what they *are* as men is damaging to women . . . Masculinity, as its critics observe, has a conspicuous limit: it cannot see beyond itself.

These difficulties notwithstanding, there are examples of relatively privileged groups who have used their positions to work with oppressed people for social justice. Consider, for instance, the white men and women who have formed anti-slavery organizations, worked for liberation movements like the African National Congress, supported the American civil rights movement, and taught counterracist curricula in their classrooms (Douglas 1994). And as Kimmel (1992) has documented, there are some men who individually and collectively have swam "against the tide" by supporting women's push for full citizenship.

As I will argue in chapter 2, neither men nor women are monolithic categories; they are divided by social class, age, sexual and ethnic/racial backgrounds. Since profeminism involves a male-positive position, it is important not to posit an "us versus them" research agenda in which "Men are reduced to a gender with no redeeming qualities and women [are] regarded as blameless in the maintenance of gender-stratified societies" (Davis 1994, 236). Thus it is vital to emphasize that a given man may not be a rapist. Nevertheless, all men live in a *rape culture* that is constituted by a constellation of signs, ideologies, and images that legitimize men's violence against women. By analogy, although individual white men and women in Australia and the United States may not be racists, they live in a racist culture. And just as white people have a fundamental role to play in eliminating racism, men have the capacity to eradicate sexism. This is why it is imperative to counter the conventional wisdom of the men's rights and mythopoetic movements that men are "oppressed" by women. It is undeniable that some men do experience confusion, unease, anger, threat, betrayal, and pain. But this angst-ridden situation has been caused not by women, but by an ensemble of competitive and hierarchical practices that enable relatively privileged men to oppress both women and subordinated and marginalized men. To equate men's emotional confusion with the everyday harassment, assault, and violence against women is a profound misuse of the term "oppression" (Clatterbaugh 1992). Radford Ruether (1993, 16) has felicitously pointed out the irony of this reactionary discourse of some sections of the men's movement by comparing it with race relations in the United States:

Let us imagine a parallel "white people's movement" aris-
ing that would claim to solve racism by seeing it as a
problem of the wounded white psyche. We are told that
white people are deeply wounded by the lack of positive
white role models, exacerbated by the vicious criticism
of white people that took place during in the civil rights
and the apartheid movements. It is acknowledged that
white people have sometimes been immature in and have
used their power aggressively, but this is only because
they were insecure in their whiteness. What is needed is
to restore white people's confidence in whiteness as a
manifestation of strong and positive psychic traits.

PROFEMINIST RESEARCH AND SPORT

Gender inequalities are systematic at all levels of sport. At
the elite level men compete in nearly double the number of
events as women at the summer Olympics; about 25 percent of
countries competing at the summer Olympics, mainly Muslim
ones, send no women representatives; only seven of the 94
members of the IOC are women and only six of the 174
national Olympic associations in the world have women pres-
idents (Hall 1995). At the grass roots level virtually every
study of sport in liberal-democratic states has found that vast
gender imbalances exist. The following Australian findings
are typical of most advanced industrial nations:

- girls have lower levels of fitness than boys
- girls drop out of sport and physical activity at an earlier
  age than boys
- more girls than boys have negative attitudes towards sport
  and physical activity
- more girls than boys have low self-concepts about their bodily abilities
- women are more unlikely than men to return to sport later
  in life

- women are immensely underrepresented in coaching and administrative positions
- there are only a handful of women sports journalists
- less than 2 percent of media coverage is given to women's sport (ASC 1992).

Despite being lauded as a vital constructor of moral integrity and discipline, sport can engender blind obedience to figures of authority, override personal autonomy, and lead to "overconformity" to group norms both on and off the field (Curry 1991; Hughes and Coakley 1991; Williams and Taylor 1994). Like other tightly-knit competitive male groups (e.g., military units, gangs, college fraternities), sport often produces "groupthink"—a mind-set that makes men incapable of believing that there is anything wrong with their harassing, abusive, and violent behavior toward women. Examples of "groupthink" in sport are evident in the burgeoning incidents of sexual harassment and violence involving male coaches and athletes (Crossett et al. 1995; Curry 1991; Fritner and Rubinson 1993; Kane and Disch 1993; Katz 1995; Koss and Gaines 1993; Lenskyj 1992a; Melnick 1992; Messner and Sabo 1994; White et al. 1992; William and Taylor 1994). Recent studies of U.S. college campuses have shown that:

- one third of sexual assaults on women involve athletes
- athletes are the second largest group after fraternity members to commit gang rapes
- women are particularly reluctant to press charges against male athletes because of the hallowed status they have in society.

In 1993, three white, middle class high school football players in Newark, New Jersey, were convicted of first-degree sexual assault on a slightly retarded 17-year-old woman, and another, on whom the woman performed fellatio, was found guilty of fourth-degree sexual assault. While nine other boys cheered, the athletes, two of whom were team co-captains, assaulted the woman with a miniature baseball bat and broomstick. In another case, rape charges were laid against fifteen white, middle class high school athletes from Lakewood, California, who called themselves the "Spur Posse," after their favorite professional basketball team, the San Antonio Spurs. When the boys were released from jail they received a hero's welcome. On national television programs, some of the boys bragged about how gang members earned "spurs," or "points," for raping girls as young as ten. One boasted that about a third of his 67 victims had been virgins, and crowed, "When ya got it, ya got it." A school physical education teacher claimed the incident had been "blown out of proportion"; the athletes were described as "red-blooded boys who will be boys" and the girls were called "sluts"; a father of one of the accused maintained that the "Spur Posse" was "no different from the band, the choir or the PTA." All but one of the 15 boys were subsequently acquitted (Wenzel 1993, 3). In 1995, a former British Olympic swimming coach was sentenced to seventeen years in prison for two rapes and eleven indecent assaults on young female swimmers over a 15-year period. Lenskyj (1993) has documented a case in which a Canadian coach who raped a paraplegic athlete ten years ago is still coaching young women. The revelations of chronic wife abuse by former American football heroes Vance Johnson, Warren Moon, and O.J. Simpson ought to shatter any illusions there still might be about the character-building virtues of sport.

To reiterate the general point made above, I believe that given these facts, profeminist men should use their relatively privileged position to study men's power and privileges in sporting contexts.

SUMMARY

I have argued that profeminist men can assume a stance analogous to members of relatively privileged ethnic and racial groups who use their powerful positions to research ethnic and racial prejudice and discrimination. So, just as relatively privileged white feminists can combat racism among women (Ang 1995), relatively privileged men can oppose sexism among men (hooks 1984). This line of investigation has not usually been on the agenda of most academic men, as they are unlikely to see that there is anything problematic about their power and privileges. In an article entitled "Invisible Masculinity" (1993), Kimmel contends that American men—or more accurately, white, middle class heterosexual men—have no history. He argues that although men have been conspicuous as athletes, politicians, scientists, and soldiers, they generally have been indiscernible *as men*. As Kimmel (1993, 30) notes, this veiled status of men is one of the principal vectors of power and privilege in society:

> The very processes that confer privilege to one group and not to another are often invisible to those upon whom that privilege is conferred . . . men have come to think of themselves as genderless, in part because they can afford the luxury of ignoring the centrality of gender . . . Invisibility reproduces inequality. And the invisibility of gender to those privileged by it reproduces the inequalities that are circumscribed by gender.

A major aim of this book is to use empirical research to make hegemonic masculinity "visible"—to articulate men's identities and power *as men* in organizations that they generally assume are genderless. This seems like a self-evident goal until it is recognized just how little attention scholars have paid to it in their empirical research. Although men are usually mentioned as being theoretically important by scholars working in the "women and management" research tradition, they seldom have been included at the empirical level. Research from the more recent "men and management" perspective has been primarily theoretical, and few of the meagre empirical studies have included women. Although feminist scholars have examined gender inequalities in management in sporting organizations, most research has consisted of survey research. There have been virtually no comparisons of the everyday practices that men *and* women use to "manage" gender and no studies that have used profeminist and social constructionist perspectives. Thus, a major strength of this book is that it compares the managerial experiences of both men and women in a particularly androcentric organizational culture.

It is hoped that this effort will help other men to acknowledge the structural privileges and power we hold in organizational life and how we might use our collective resources to "engender" justice. This is not a case of taking the high moral ground, but as Starhawk (1993, 29) argues, of encouraging men to confront their complicity in sustaining relations of inequality between men and women, and to take personal and collective responsibility for liberating themselves rather than blaming women for their problems:

> A men's movement I could trust would be clear about the difference between spiritual malaise and oppression. Oppression is what slaves suffer; malaise is what happens to the slave owners whose personalities are warped and whose essential humanity is necessarily undermined by their position. Malaise and oppression are both painful, but they are not comparable. And the necessary first step in the cure for what ails the slave owner is to free the slave. If men want to be liberated, they must first be willing to let go of the institutionalized advantage they have in every arena of society.

NOTE

1. Corporate director Gary Pemberton was eventually selected as "Mr. Right." Pemberton resigned in 1996 and since then three other men have occupied the chief executive position on the Sydney Organizing Committee for the 2000 Olympics (SOCOG). Sallyanne Atkinson, the woman who was belatedly appointed to the organizing

committee, resigned in 1994. Former union leader, Anna Booth, who was appointed in 1995, is the only woman on the SOCOG board. In February 1997, SOCOG appointed corporate consultant Glen-Marie Frost as head of its community and corporate relations division. Frost's appointment was greeted in mainly condescending ways by print journalists. *The Sydney Morning Herald* covered her appointment with the headline "City Socialite to be the New Face of SOCOG." Although mentioning Frost's business experience, reporter Matthew Moore also described her appointment as a "surprise," and noted that she was "a former beauty queen and model" who was "well-known on the luncheon circuit" (Moore 1997:6). Similarly, *The Australian* proclaimed: "Socialite Wins Olympic PR Job," and reporter John Ellicot described Frost as "a Sydney socialite best known to the public as the face of the Bankcard marketing campaign in the 1970s" (Ellicot 1997:3).

Two

Theoretical Framework

THINKING INSTITUTIONALLY ABOUT
GENDER AND ORGANIZATIONS

CONSIDER THE FOLLOWING WAYS in which gender is embedded in organizations on a global basis:

- the marked sex-segregation of labor forces, with men likely to be in powerful, well-paying, permanent positions and women in low-status, low-paying, casual ones;
- the regimes of homophobia and heterosexual coupledom that govern organizational life;
- pervasive assumptions that the average employee is a male breadwinner for his housewife and nuclear family;
- conventional representations of organizations in advertisements, which portray women as sex objects and men as authority figures;
- rigid sexual differences in dress and appearance;
- the gendered nature of conversations, jokes, and insults;
- systematic sexual harassment of women by men; and
- predominantly masculine definitions of merit, skill, and performance.

These *institutionalized* patterns mean that organizations cannot be analyzed in a gender-neutral way. To the contrary, gender must be seen as decisive in organizations because most have cultures in which men's experiences are ascendant and women's are subordinate. In short, organizations are key sites where gender struggles take place and in which femininities and masculinities are both constructed and reproduced. In order to conceptualize these institutionalized, gendered dynamics of organizational life, it is necessary to use a social constructionist framework.

GENDER AND SOCIAL CONSTRUCTIONISM

Social constructionists emphasize the diverse types of masculinities, femininities, and gender systems that have existed throughout history (cf. Herdt 1994; Lorber and Farrell 1991; Sanday 1981; Weeks 1985). According to social constructionists, gender relations and identities are not the "natural" outcome of biology or the product of "appropriate" sex-role socialization, but rather institutionalized *practices* that all of us "do" (West and Zimmerman 1987). Given that men control the most powerful social institutions, and their values are more highly esteemed than women's, then women must continually "do" gender under disadvantaged conditions. Kandiyoti (1988, 286) uses the term *patriarchal bargains* to refer to the fluid and tension-ridden ways in which both men and women "accommodate and acquiesce" to preexisting gendered structures and meanings, even though women generally "bargain from a weaker position."

GENDERED STRUCTURES OF LABOR, POWER, AND CATHEXIS

Connell has outlined one of the most sophisticated approaches to the social construction of gender relations and identities. He suggests that we need to examine how articulations between the macrolevel *gender order* and microlevel *gender regimes* (e.g., religion, sport, work, the state, the media, family life) are underpinned by structures of labor, power, and cathexis.

Structures of Labor

The vertical and horizontal segregation of labor structures is particularly evident in the high ratio of women in occupations with relatively low levels of authority, prestige, and remuneration, as well as their disproportionate contribution to unpaid domestic labor and caregiving. These gendered divisions are especially pronounced in managerial occupations, where generally less than 5 percent of women, mostly from Anglo backgrounds, have made it beyond the "glass ceiling" and become senior administrators (Woldring 1996). Most are concentrated in "velvet ghettos" (e.g., affirmative action, public relations, human resource management) that are stereotyped as "women's work" (Davidson and Cooper 1992, 1994; Fagenson 1993; Powell 1993; Tanton 1994). Liff and Wajcman (1995, 90–91) cite a major British study on women managers that begins by stating that, "a visitor from Mars could be forgiven for thinking that management jobs have been specifically designed for men married to full-time wives and mothers who shoulder the burden of family life." According to Antal and Izraeli (1993, 63), "probably the single most important hurdle for women in management in all industrialized countries is the persistent stereotype that associates management with being male."

In Australia, women constitute 42 percent of the labor force but only 25 percent of all managers, 14 percent of specialist managers, and less than 5 percent of senior managers. The majority of women managers are located in service industries and earn on average about 25 percent less than their male counterparts. Only 3 percent of the nearly 1,300 directors in the 168 public and private sector organizations are women, and none of the top 500 companies has a woman CEO. There are no women on the management boards of Australia's top ten companies and women constitute just 13 percent of the members of public service boards (Bellamy and Ramsay 1994; Carruthers 1997; HRSCLCA 1992; Karpin 1995; Still 1993; Vilkinas 1991).

Under 3 percent of New Zealand women who work full-time are in administrative or managerial positions, and most of these are Anglos (James and Saville-Smith 1992). In their survey of nearly 200 of New Zealand's top companies, McGregor et al. (1994, 4) reported that:

> The study reveals a dismal picture of women in decision-making positions . . . at every level of management women are substantially under-represented, under-paid and there is little incentive for women to press on towards senior management . . . despite New Zealand passing equal pay legislation in the seventies and progressive equal opportunity initiatives in the public sector since then, slow progress appears to have been made by women in management in *both* the public and private sectors.

A 1991 survey found the following percentages of women in senior management positions in the top 250 Canadian companies: industrial, 6.1 percent, crown corporations, 5.6 percent, financial services, 7.9 percent, insurance, 14.2 percent, and other, 5.9 percent (Allan 1991). A comprehensive study of the Canadian public service reported that only 12 percent of its senior managers were women (Ministry of Supply and Services 1991).

Structures of Power

Men control most sites of organized coercion and surveillance in society (e.g., the police, military, judiciary) and perpetrate most of the violence against both women and other men. The vast majority of sexual assaults against women are perpetrated by men, most of whom are friends or relatives of their victims. Thus, it is absolutely crucial to view sexual assault and harassment not as the random acts of psychopathic individuals, but as the "normal" behavior of men who accept aggression, intimidation, and violence as a rightful and necessary aspect of their relationships with women.

This "iron fist" is complemented by an ideological "velvet glove" that "persuades" both men and women that the ascendancy of men's values, interests, and privileges is both natural and legitimate. Connell uses the concepts *hegemonic masculinity* and *emphasized femininity* to describe this form of cultural power. The former term refers to the "culturally idealized form of masculine character," which associates masculinity with "toughness and competitiveness," the "subordination of women," and "the marginalization of gay men" (Connell 1990b, 83, 94). Although this type of masculinity may not be the most common, many men consent to its ideals:

> The public face of hegemonic masculinity is not necessarily what powerful men are, but what sustains their power and what large numbers of men are motivated to support. The notion of "hegemony" generally implies a large measure of consent. Few men are Bogarts or Stallones, but many collaborate in sustaining those images. (Connell 1987, 184)

Emphasized femininity is defined by the accommodation of women to "the interests and desires of men" and "women's compliance with this subordination," while other forms of femininity "are defined by complex strategic combinations of resistance and co-operation" (Connell 1987, 183–184). Connell suggests that there is "a kind of 'fit' between hegemonic masculinity and emphasized femininity" in that "hegemonic masculinity must embody a successful collective strategy in relation to women." However, the intricacy of gender relations means that:

> . . . no simple strategy is possible: a "mix" is necessary. So hegemonic masculinity can contain at the same time, quite consistently, openings towards domesticity and openings towards violence, towards misogyny and towards heterosexual attraction. (1987, 185–186)

Structures of Cathexis

Cathexis is defined as "sexual social relationships" that "are organized around one person's emotional attachments to another" (Connell 1987, 111–112). The dominant pattern of desire in capitalist societies is based on binary, hierarchical sexual difference and heterosexual coupledom. Yet Connell stresses that cathectic attachments are not fully explained by sexual difference because heterosexual women are sexualized to an extent that heterosexual men are not: "the erotic reciprocity in hegemonic heterosexuality is based on unequal exchange" (Connell 1987, 113). He emphasizes that hegemonic heterosexuality is replete with internal tensions, interweaves uneasily with homosexuality, is constantly challenged, and has to be continually defended and reasserted.

It is vital to recognize that although labor, power, and cathexis can be analytically separated, these three structures intertwine differently depending on the context. Connell argues that these interlacing structures are always comprised of complex combinations of physical and economic coercion and hegemony: "The authority of men is not spread in an even blanket across every department of social life" (1987, 109). Thus, relations of power are neither static nor uncontested: some men and women do struggle against the oppressive structures that constrain their everyday practices. However, dissenters have to contend with both men who have a vested interest in sustaining hegemonic masculinities and with women who are complicit in sustaining the emphasized femininities that help to reproduce gender inequalities. Connell stresses that these elaborate gender formations interact in multifarious and uneven ways with other social divisions (e.g., class, ethnicity, race, age). He also stresses the importance of grasping the "interplay" of labor, power, and cathexis at the local and global levels:

We must distinguish the *global* or macro relationships of power in which women are subordinated to men in the society as a whole from the micro situation in particular households, particular workplaces, particular settings. It is possible for the local patterns to depart from the global pattern, even to contradict it. (Connell 1987, 111)

In summary, Connell's theory of gender relations and identities as *complex structuring processes* focuses on institutionalized arrangements both between and among men and women. Relations at both the macro and micro levels are characterized by obdurate, hierarchical, and exploitative structures that set limits on how gender is "done." Connell emphasizes that although there is no "ultimate determinant," there is "a unity . . . an orderliness, which needs to be understood . . . not the unity of a *system* [but] a unity—always imperfect and under construction—of historical composition . . . a matter of the real historical process of interaction and group formation" (Connell 1987, 116).

Connell avoids the ahistorical, deterministic, and essentialist traps of conceptualizing men and women as possessors of immutable traits by accentuating multiple sources of gendered power and the contradictory and historically specific ways in which gender relations are asymmetrically structured. Although Connell stresses that structure constrains practice, he insists that practice also influences structure. It is this point that allows him to highlight that although gender relations and identities are socially constructed, they also are fluid and hence capable of transformation. Connell's approach also averts the androcentrism, Eurocentrism, and crude relativism associated with some postmodernist and postfeminist approaches to social theory and gender (cf. Ebert 1992–93; Franklin et al. 1991; Hall 1985; Jackson 1992; Mouzelis 1993; Walby 1992; West 1989). Some of the intricate ways in which structures of labor, power, and cathexis interface are illustrated in Table 2.1.

IMPLICATIONS FOR GENDER AND SPORT

There is increasing recognition of the cardinal role sporting practices play in constructing gender relations and identities.

TABLE 2.1
Ideal-type Representation of Connell's Structures of
Labor, Power, and Cathexis at the Macro Level*

Gender Order of Society

Labor	*Power*	*Cathexis*
Occupational segregation	Institutionalized "triad of violence" by men against themselves, other men, and women	Institutionalized heterosexual coupledom
Links between segregation, profitability, and labor control	Men's control of state apparatuses, the police the legal system, and the military	Institutionalized homophobia
Exclusion of women from accumulating wealth or attaining a secure career position	Articulations between hegemonic masculinity and emphasized femininity	Sexualization and objectification of women
Maintenance of sexual demarcations through work practices that reinforce male solidarity		
Women's disproportionate responsibility for child care		

Source: R. W. Connell, *Masculinities* (Sydney: Allen & Unwin, 1995), and *Gender and Power* (Sydney: Allen & Unwin, 1987).

For example, Trujillo (1991, 292) claims that, "Perhaps no single institution in American culture has influenced our sense of masculinity more than sport"—an observation that is also relevant to most other countries. Elsewhere, I have argued that social constructionism, particularly Connell's approach, can be useful for empirically analyzing gender relations and identities in sport, as well as how gender regimes in sport interact with other social divisions such as class, race, age, region, nation, and sexuality (Boyle and McKay 1995; McKay 1992b;

20

1993, 1995; McKay and Huber 1992; McKay and Smith 1995).
In Australia, Canada, and New Zealand, sport has been crucial in constructing hegemonic masculinity and marginalizing women and gay men, especially through falsely universalizing victories by men in international competitions like the America's Cup (Australia), ice hockey (Canada), and rugby union (New Zealand) as the embodiment of a unified, heterosexual nation (Gruneau and Whitson 1994; Hall et al. 1991; McKay 1991; McKay and Middlemiss 1995; Nauright 1995). Some sporting organizations in all three countries limit full membership status to men and only accept women as associates. This means that men dominate executive positions, voting rights, and budgets, and regulate women's access to bars, equipment, and facilities. Women members also perform a disproportionate share of ancillary activities such as providing food and refreshments, cleaning, fund-raising, and redecorating. Women frequently act as chauffeurs, cooks, laundresses, secretaries, and cheerleaders—tasks that men seldom perform, especially *for* women (Bennett 1990; Boyle and McKay 1995; Cameron 1996; Davis 1990; Thompson 1990, 1992).

The gendered division of managerial occupations in general is also manifest in sporting organizations. Vertical segregation is evident in the meager number of women in senior managerial positions in national sporting organizations (NSOs) (see Table 2.2). Horizontal segregation is manifest in the different types of managerial tasks that men and women perform and the dearth of women in core managerial areas (see Table 2.3). In Table 2.4 I have indicated how Connell's analytical framework can be applied to the gender regime of sport in an abstract way. Messner's (1990b, 213) description of American football provides an apposite example of the interrelationship among labor, power, and cathexis in sport:

> Football, based as it is on the most extreme possibilities of the male body . . . is clearly a world apart from women, who are relegated to the role of cheerleaders/sex objects

TABLE 2.2
Percent of Women Executive Directors of NSOs
in Australia, Canada, and New Zealand*

Country	Percent of Women Executive Directors
Australia	16
Canada	26
New Zealand	11

*Source: Reprinted with permission from J. Cameron, "Women Who Manage: Study of Volunteer National Sports Administrators." (Christchurch Sociology Department, University of Canterbury, 1994.)

TABLE 2.3
Ideal-type Representation of Gender Structure of Core and
Peripheral Management Areas in Sporting Organizations

Gender Structure	Core Areas	Peripheral Areas
Male-dominated	Finance Marketing Policy planning Talent identification Sports science Elite sports Olympic sports Men's events	Anomalous combination, except for overrepresentation of men coaching elite women's teams
Female-dominated	Anomalous combination	Affirmative action Youth sports People with disabilities Women's events Human resources Public relations

on the sidelines . . . in contrast to the bare and vulnerable bodies of the cheerleaders, the armored bodies of the football players are elevated to mythical status, and as such, give testimony to the undeniable "fact" that here is at least one place where men are clearly superior to women.

TABLE 2.4
General Examples of Structures of Labor, Power, and Cathexis
in the Gender Regime of Sport

Labor	*Power*	*Cathexis*
Women's dispropor-tionate share of ancillary sporting labor (e.g., providing food and transport, cleaning, fund-raising)	Media's symbolic glorification of men's sport and symbolic annihilation of women's sport	Heterosexual coupling between male athletes and female cheerleaders
Absence and underrepresentation of women in playing, coaching, officiating, administrative, reporting, and ownership positions	Exaltation of sporting activities based on competition, strength, intimidation, and violence	Intensely homophobic nature of sporting subcultures
	Sexual harassment of women athletes and reporters	

Source: M. Boyle and J. McKay, "'You Leave Your Troubles at the Gate': A Case Study of the Exploitation of Older Women's Labor and Leisure." *Gender & Society* 9 (1995): 556–575.

SUMMARY

In this chapter I have outlined how Connell's social construc-tionist perspective can be used to analyze gender relations and identities in sporting organizations. In subsequent chap-ters I use this framework to investigate affirmative action ini-tiatives by the state in sport, patterns of labor, power, and cathexis in sporting organizations, managers' perceptions of affirmative action, media representations of affirmative action in sport, and the gender politics of doing research on affirma-tive action policy.

Three

The Corporate-Managerial State, Gender, and Sport

UNTIL ABOUT THIRTY YEARS AGO, most amateur sporting organizations in Australia, Canada, and New Zealand were subject
to minimal direct regulation by the state. Most organizations
were administered by *dilettante* "old boys" and relied heavily
on grass-roots support. Today, all three countries have multi-
million dollar state agencies which are responsible for the
national planning and funding of amateur sport, including
affirmative action programs. Increasing numbers of amateur
sporting organizations have CEOs and managers for advertising, marketing, and public relations, and are dependent on
either the private and/or state sector for support (Berrett 1993;
Collins and Stuart 1994; Hall et al. 1991; Hindson et al. 1994;
McKay et al. 1993). However, much of this intervention
occurred under the aegis of traditional welfare state regimes
that have been displaced by austere policies inimical with
affirmative action. Therefore, it is imperative to ascertain the
articulations among gender, the corporate-managerial state,
and affirmative action policies in sport.

The ability of corporations to transcend national boundaries means that the economies of Australia, Canada, and
New Zealand have been drawn inexorably into the "global traf-
fic" in people, goods, and services (Larner 1993; McBride and
Shields 1993; Yeatman 1990). For about the past three
decades, this trend has presented acute fiscal and legitimation
crises for the governments of these three countries because of

their semiperipheral status in the international economy. Faced with high levels of unemployment, protracted economic recessions, pressure from international monetary agencies, fluctuating commodity prices on global markets, high rates of foreign ownership, rising current account deficits, and the exponentially increasing demands that citizens have placed on the state, both liberal and conservative governments have attempted to "roll back" traditional welfare regimes by implementing policies based on neoclassical economics. Governments have attempted to reduce the purported waste involved in state-funded programs and emulate the allegedly more accountable, efficient, and effective practices of the corporate sector by promoting privatization, corporatization, and deregulation (cf. Albo et al. 1993; Bell and Head 1994; Boston et al. 1991; Du Plessis 1995; Johnson et al. 1994; Kelsey 1993; Pusey 1991). This strategy has been designed to assist underperforming national labor forces to compete more effectively in international markets—often encapsulated by the hackneyed sporting aphorism of "competing on a level playing field."

These measures have also been part of a qualitative shift from public *service* to public *management* in the state sector. Public service managers have developed fetishes for strategic plans, mission statements, targets, and performance indicators; metaphors like "lean and mean machine," and "the bottom line" have become rampant; and terms like "clients," "stakeholders," "corporate excellence," "restructuring," "total quality management," "market share," and "enterprise culture" are used in a mantra-like fashion (du Gay 1991; Hood 1995; Keat and Abercrombie 1990; Miller and Rose 1993; Rees 1994; Willmott 1993).

AFFIRMATIVE ACTION IN THE CORPORATE-MANAGERIAL STATE

Affirmative action initiatives in Australia, Canada, and New Zealand have emanated almost entirely from the state sector, and all three nations have extensive bureaucracies that oversee affirmative action and related schemes (e.g., equal opportunity, equity, human rights, social justice). These countries contain considerable numbers of influential middle- and high-ranking "femocrats" who lobby and advise politicians and state functionaries on affirmative action.

But there is a profound tension between these commitments to affirmative action and the regimes of masculinity and economic rationalism that are ascendant in both the public and private spheres. For instance, conservative parties in Canada and New Zealand have cut back an array of programs that directly affect women's lives, while the importance of "traditional family values" has been a pervasive motif among all the major parties in Australia (Burt 1993; Du Plessis 1992; Else 1992; Hyman 1994; Johnson 1993). Promulgation of affirmative action is restricted almost entirely to the public sector, and there are paltry penalties for non-compliance. Issuing a grievance involves both financial and psychological stress, and relatively powerless individuals usually have to make their complaints stick against powerful organizations. Affirmative action agencies in all three countries bear almost total responsibility for monitoring compliance and dealing with complaints, an increasing number of which involve "reverse discrimination" claims by men (Wieneke 1992). Although a few companies are renowned for their affirmative action programs, the private sector has been largely indifferent or hostile to affirmative action initiatives. Moreover, within the current corporate-managerial regimes of the state, "Equal opportunity . . . comes to be reframed in terms of what it can do to improve management, not what it can do to develop the conditions of social justice and democratic citizenship" (Yeatman 1990, 16). Consider, for instance, the following comments in *Enterprising Nation*, a landmark report on how the government should exploit Australia's diverse labor force more strategically:

> Capitalising on the talents of diversity involves half our population—women—and we must also utilise the skills of

our multicultural society. Major improvements in management skills can be effected simply by opening up equal opportunities for these under-utilised groups to attain the senior levels of corporate management. (Karpin 1995, 11)

Similar sentiments are evident in a Canadian government report on barriers to women's advancement in the federal public service, which stated that the aging nature of the civil service and the changing demographics of the work force would compel the government to recruit and employ more women. The authors claimed that unless barriers to women's advancement were diminished, the civil service "will not be able to attract and retain capable, well-educated women, for whom they will have to compete with a private sector that already recognizes the challenge it faces in securing the necessary work force in the next decade" (Ministry of Supply and Services 1991, 123).

I suggest that the patterns described above make it difficult to refer to any monolithic "patriarchal state" in Australia, Canada, or New Zealand (cf. Armstrong 1992; Burt 1993; Du Plessis 1992; Pringle and Watson 1992; Sawer 1994; Yeatman 1994). For instance, all three countries have antifeminist women's groups which have had varying degrees of success in pressuring the state to resist even liberal-feminist agendas. However, to say that gender relations have become more intricate in various state arenas does not obviate the immense power differences between men and women. I submit that corporate-managerialism has been interleaved with elements of instrumental rationality, surveillance, discipline, social Darwinism, and possessive individualism—the very features that have been key components of hegemonic masculinity in advanced capitalist societies (cf. Brown 1992; Collinson and Hearn 1994; Kerfoot and Knights 1993; Winter and Roberts 1980). It is useful, therefore, to view struggles over affirmative action as taking place in a context in which *patriarchal-welfare* state formations are being supplanted by *corporate-managerial* ones (see Table 3.1).

TABLE 3.1
Ideal-type Comparison of Discourses in Patriarchal-Welfare and
Corporate-Managerial State Formations in Liberal-Democracies*

Patriarchal-Welfare State	*Corporate-Managerial State*
Backgrounds of Managerial Elites	
Privileged Anglo Men	Privileged Anglo men; a few privileged Anglo women; and a few non-Anglo men and women
Broadly educated in arts, humanities, and social sciences	Narrowly educated in neoclassical economics
Political Discourses of Managerial Elites	
Noblesse oblige	Social Darwinism
Liberal to liberal-democratic	Neoliberal to neoconservative
Administrative Discourses of Managerial Elites	
Public service/administration	Corporate management
Protection of domestic markets from international competition	Deregulation of domestic markets for competition in the global market ('the level playing field')
Benthamite—state shapes economic and civil spheres	Economic rationalism—market discipline shapes state and civil spheres ("society should be governed *by* business *for* business")
Gender Discourses of Managerial Elites	
Patriarchal	Patriarchal mixed with "symbolic pacification" via affirmative action programs
Equity, justice, and welfare based on male-breadwinner/housewife relationship	Equity, justice, and welfare based on "indicators" (e.g., efficiency, targets, productivity, performance)

Source: F. Castles, "Social Protection by Other Means; Australia's Strategy of Coping with External Vulnerability." In *The Comparative History of Public Policy*, edited by F. Castles (Oxford: Polity Press, 1989).

R. W. Connell, "The State, Gender and Sexual Politics: Theory and Appraisal." *Theory and Society* 19(1990): 507–544.

(continued on next page)

TABLE 3.1 *(continued from last page)*

J. Kenway, "Feminist Theories of the State: To be or not to be?" In *Society, State and Politics in Australia*, edited by M. Muetzelfeldt (Sydney: Pluto, 1992).

C. Pateman, "The Patriarchal Welfare State." In *Democracy and the Welfare State*, edited by H. Gutmann (Princeton: Princeton University Press, 1988).

M. Pusey, *Economic Rationalism in Canberra: A Nation-building State Changes its Mind* (London: Cambridge University Press, 1991).

A Yeatman, *Bureaucrats, Technocrats, Femocrats: Essays on the Contemporary Australian State* (Sydney: Allen and Unwin, 1990).

IMPLICATIONS FOR AFFIRMATIVE ACTION IN SPORT

In 1972 the U.S. federal government passed Title IX of the Education Amendments Act to redress the enormous gender inequities in intercollegiate and interscholastic sports. Since then many other liberal-democratic states have followed suit by implementing policies designed to eliminate or mitigate discrimination against women in sport. This usually has entailed establishing women's sport promotion units, introducing special training schemes for women coaches and administrators, pressuring the media to cover more women's sport and to present "positive images" of sportswomen, and obtaining more corporate funding. Australia, Canada, and New Zealand have state-sponsored women's programs of this kind.

Canada

Direct management of Canadian amateur sport by the federal state began with the creation of the Fitness and Amateur Sport Directorate and the National Advisory Council on Fitness and Amateur Sport in 1961. This move was part of a strategy to improve standards and enhance Canada's image at a time when Eastern bloc states were making quantum improvements in international sport due to their intensive talent identification and training methods. However, performances did not increase satisfactorily, so the Canadian Olympic Association and the federal and provincial governments instituted high performance programs: in 1971 Sport Canada (SC) and Recreation Canada were established within the Directorate; in 1973 the agency was upgraded to a branch status with an assistant deputy minister; and in 1976 the first federal minister with responsibilities for fitness and amateur sport was appointed. In 1977 Recreation Canada became Fitness and Recreation Canada, but in 1980 the federal government handed over responsibility for recreation to the provinces and directed most of its policies toward high performance sport. Kidd (1988) states that by the time of the Commonwealth Games in Edmonton in 1978, the government's strategy was being referred to as an attempt to make Canada the "GDR of the Commonwealth." In 1983 SC established "Best Ever," a program that was designed to help winter Olympic sports to prepare for the 1988 Olympic Games in Calgary. This scheme, which was eventually called "quadrennial planning," was then extended to all Olympic sports, and finally to virtually all NSOs. Under the conservative Mulroney regime, the Sports Marketing Council was established in order to obtain corporate support for "Best Ever."

The rationalization and commodification of amateur sport has shifted federal policies away from a broad concern with both recreational and high performance sport to a narrow focus on the latter (Harvey et al. 1995; Kidd 1995). Consequently, there have been qualitative changes in the operations and composition of NSOs:

> . . . a move away from their traditional design type, that is, an organization controlled by volunteers and operated relatively informally with professional help, to a new organizational design type an organization which was highly structured along bureaucratic lines controlled by professionals with volunteer help. (Slack and Hinings 1994, 808)

When Canadian sprinter Ben Johnson tested positive for using anabolic steroids at the 1988 Olympics, the government launched an extensive inquiry into sport. The 1990 Dubin Report was highly critical of what it termed the government's "medals, flags and national anthem" stance toward sport, and recommended a strategy that was more inclusive of women and people with disabilities. The government responded by releasing a series of documents that attempted to address the criticisms made in the Dubin document. In 1992 the federal minister for sport presented a task force report that contained more than 100 recommendations and recognized the need to include more women and people with disabilities (Semotiuk 1994).

Ann Hall (1994, 1995), who has had a long involvement in women's sport in Canada both as an academic and grass roots feminist, maintains that early government intervention was characterized by indifference or hostility toward sportswomen's needs. However, a Women's Program was established in the Fitness and Amateur Sport Directorate in 1980, and the following year a small group of activists formed the Canadian Association for the Advancement of Women and Sport (CAAWS). This organization was supported by SC's Women's Program until 1984, when it began receiving most of its funds from the Secretary of State Women's Program. In 1986 the government released a major report which detailed its official commitment to equal opportunity for women. In 1994 the manager of the Women's Program resigned and her responsibilities were subsumed by a manager in the Policy, Planning, and Evaluation Unit. As this book was going to press, a new manager of the Women's Program had still not been appointed.

In their study of policy-making processes in Canadian NSOs, Macintosh and Whitson (1990) reported that most managers perceived barriers to women's participation to lie outside of sport and that affirmative action policies impeded the development of elite performance. Despite some constructive moves by SC, its meager financial and moral commitments to affirmative action gave executives of NSOs a justification for also assigning a low priority to it:

... the federal government's emphasis on high-performance sport, and its preoccupation with institutionalizing a performance support system capable of preparing elite Canadian athletes to compete successfully in international sport, have undercut the pursuit of equity-related objectives. (Whitson and Macintosh 1990, 27–28)

New Zealand

In 1973 a major transformation of New Zealand amateur sport began when a Labour government passed the Recreation and Sport Act and created a Ministry of Recreation and Sport and the New Zealand Council for Recreation and Sport. Hindson et al. (1994) suggest that these initiatives heralded a shift in state responsibilities from building facilities toward promoting local and national programs. A Labour government in 1984 embarked on a policy of privatization that had direct implications for sport. Following the issuance of two major reports in 1985, a new version of the Recreation and Sport Act was passed in 1987, which resulted in the Ministry of Recreation and Sport and the Council for Recreation and Sport being replaced by the Hillary Commission for Recreation and Sport (HC). The HC was a semi-independent, national statutory body that was given a mandate to facilitate healthy and active lifestyles for all citizens. It had 19 staff and two advisory bodies, SportsCorp and RecCorp, that were composed of eleven commissioners appointed by the minister for recreation and sport. The main task of the commissioners was to "advise the whole commission on policy in their respective areas after consultation with a wide range of related organization such as government departments, local authorities, national recreation and sports organisation, and other groups" (*First Annual Report* 1988, 5).

The election of a conservative National government in 1990 resulted in further modifications to sports policy. In 1992 the organization's name was changed to the Hillary Commission for Sport, Fitness and Leisure, and administration and funding of recreational arts was transferred away from the commission. Volkerling (1994, 8) maintains that the new nomenclature was indicative of the commission "shedding its cultural programs and acquiring a policy focus geared towards reducing social disorder and promoting national achievement." For instance, he cites the minister of recreation and sport as saying that the HC had a role to play in achieving "social and economic prosperity." Collins and Stuart (1994, 53) quote the minister as expressing the belief that a "kid in sport is a kid out of court." Gidlow et al. (1995) and Perkins et al. (1993) argue that the "demise" of passive recreation and an emphasis on sport, fitness, and physical leisure was symptomatic of the National party's broader agenda of economic rationalism in the state sector.

In 1992 SportsCorp and RecCorp were abolished and the chair of the HC declared that it had adopted a "business-like approach" (*Annual Report* 1992, 2). In 1993 the management structure was reorganized into three "focus groups"— Corporate Services, National and International Services, and Regional and Local Services. In the annual report, the HC's outgoing chair and foundation chair applauded the inversion of roles that had recently occurred between commissioners and managers:

> Procedures for strategic planning were formalised as functions of management with input from managers (as distinct from the reverse). This coincided with the management maturing into a capable, professional unit. Reporting disciplines at all levels were tightened and streamlined and the relationship between the Commissioners, reduced to nine, and staff became more business-like. (*Annual Report* 1993, 1)

The CEO reported that:

> ... the Commission maintains a rigorous market research effort, which enables it to provide successful opportunities

where they are most needed. Similarly, the partnerships which are formed with clients will also fail if there has not been close consultation and a thorough understanding of each client's operating environment. The key management objective of the 1992–93 Corporate Plan was the development of the Commission into a client-focused organisation which identifies and responds to the needs of clients. (*Annual Report* 1993, 3)

The shift from a broad to a narrow definition of recreation and sport is evident in the differences between the HC's goals in 1988 (*First Annual Report* 1988, 5):

- develop and encourage recreation and sport
- make recreation and sport accessible and available and appealing to all New Zealanders, irrespective of age, ability, or sex
- enhance the mental and physical well-being of the nation by encouraging more healthy and active lifestyles

and in 1993:

- to increase participation in sport, fitness, and leisure
- to enhance performance in sport, fitness, and leisure
- to improve the organizational infrastructure and program delivery systems for sport, fitness and leisure (*Annual Report* 1993, 5).

A report prepared for the commission by an independent group in 1994 found that some members of local authorities, NSOs, and regional sports trusts were critical of its involvement in high performance sport, feeling that its directive to increase grass roots participation was being jeopardized by an emphasis on winning gold medals (Heylen Research Centre 1994). The commission expended $(NZ)320,000 on women's sport, fitness, and leisure in 1992–93, compared to $5,148,000 for high performance sport, including $875,000 for the

Olympic and Commonwealth Games associations alone (*Annual Report* 1993, 33).

When the HC was established its women's program manager convened a national task force to produce a report on women in physical recreation and sport. A recommendation of the report was implemented in 1989, when the Women in Physical Recreation and Sport Program was created as one of the HC's "special" areas. When the HC's name was changed in 1992, the term "physical recreation" was dropped from the women's program. Bell and Hayes (1994) claim this has been detrimental because women tend to prefer recreational activities to competitive ones. They also note that the shift in emphasis from recreation to sport was similar to the changes that were made in the Canadian sport system in the 1980s. Bell and Hayes also note that an important gap in policy liaison between women and the HC occurred when the National government closed the Ministry of Women's Affairs and relocated its responsibilities to the Ministry for Social Welfare. In 1993 the contract of the manager of the woman's program was not renewed, and the area was subsequently absorbed by Regional and Local Services. Bell and Hayes (1994, 8) observe that the commission's involvement in the 1993 New Zealand Women's Suffrage Year celebrations focused on "the need for 'up-skilling' women as more effective leaders, more efficient administrators, more women-oriented marketers and more visible coaches in New Zealand sport leaders." Overall, they are critical of the HC's corporate-managerial policies:

> "Managing" women, not as a special needs group but as consumers in the leisure industry, constitutes all women as a homogeneous group with fixed and measurable choices . . . It gives the already doubly burdened woman— responsible for, and often servicing, through their paid and unpaid work, others' fitness and leisure—the *unpaid* task of organising and lobbying for their own activities. The shift from programming and promotion to policy and advocacy thinly disguises a devolution of financial respon-

sibility to people who are not trained in areas of gender equity issues, and abandons policy functions of education, research and liaison. (Bell and Hayes 1994, 15–16)

Australia

A recommendation of a task force established by the Labor government that an Australian institute of sport be established was shelved in 1975 when a conservative party with a laissez-faire policy on sport won power. However, lackluster performances by Australian athletes at the 1976 and 1980 Olympic Games led to pressure from athletes, the media, coaches, administrators, and politicians for the government to take steps that would "restore national pride." Consequently, the government opened the Australian Institute of Sport (AIS) in 1981. The AIS—often referred to as "the gold medal factory"—receives a lion's share of the sport budget and is usually legitimized on the basis that the achievements of its star athletes will cause a grass roots surge of involvement in sport, as people will be motivated to emulate their heroes' accomplishments. The AIS is staffed by a cadre of sport scientists who employ state-of-the-art technology to monitor athletes' biological and psychological conditions. The institute provides scholarships so athletes can train in modern facilities under expert coaches and compete regularly in national and international events.

Both the planning and funding of amateur sport changed dramatically under the reign of Labor governments between 1983 and 1996. The Australian Sports Commission (ASC) was created in 1984, and in 1989 it merged with the AIS. The ASC encourages the "right" kind of corporate capital to invest in sport on the basis of image and community citizenship; or, in the words of the Second Reading Speech, which introduced reforms to the ASC in Parliament, "a more professional administrative approach" (Punch 1988, 726). A similar tenor is evident in the document, *Sport To The Year 2000* (ASC 1987), which was intended to assist the commission in its policy formulations. The report begins by emphasizing that it is time to conceive of sport as an "industry" and "economy" when planning policy. A number of scenarios for possibly developing sport and its economic, political, and social functions for Australia are then listed. A particularly useful role for sport is its purported ability to elevate the fitness levels of company employees, thereby increasing productivity, improving morale, and reducing absenteeism. After cataloging the potential for economic growth in the sports industry, the consultants acknowledge that the backbone of the industry is comprised of amateur athletes and voluntary administrators. However, times have changed, and grass roots members:

> . . . need to understand that the market segmentation and diversification issues are of as much importance to them as to the government and the commercial sector. Many sporting associations have risen to the challenge. Many have changed their modus operandi to compensate for falling participation rates. Some have reorganised in order to exploit a new situation. (1990, 22)

The apogee of the ASC's corporate-managerial discourse occurred at its 1992 Maintaining the Momentum Conference, a self-congratulatory national symposium attended by about 200 sports administrators. One of the keynote speakers was Herb Elliott, a former Olympic and world record holder in track, an ASC Board member, and the general manager of Puma Australia.* Photographs of Elliott have recently appeared in popular magazines in the "Membership has its Privileges" advertisements of American Express. After criticizing the unprofessional standards of Australian sports administrators, Elliott delivered his managerial maxim, which quickly became the conference mantra: "If you can't measure it, you can't manage it!"

The Australian Labor Party has attempted to use affirmative action policy and legislation as a way of facilitating

---

* Elliott later became president of Puma North America. In 1997 he became the Australian Olympic Committee's director of athlete and corporate relations, a position which included responsibilities for the 2000 Olympics.

equality for women. However, affirmative action in sport has come under public scrutiny only fairly recently. I now examine the gender politics surrounding some key events in these recent affirmative action initiatives. Following Pringle and Watson (1992, 70), I focus on contingencies, complexities, and pluralities, and view the state as "a diverse set of discursive arenas which play a crucial role in organizing relations of power."

In February 1991 the House of Representatives Standing Committee on Legal and Constitutional Affairs (HRSCLCA) and the ASC jointly held the Equity for Women in Sport Seminar at Parliament House in Canberra. The seminar, equivalent to a U.S. Senate inquiry, was one of a series conducted by the committee in its inquiry into equal status and equal opportunity for Australian women. The committee published nineteen volumes of submissions and a mass of other material, including the proceedings of the seminar, a related discussion paper, and the inquiry's final report. The ASC and the federal Human Rights and Equal Opportunity Commission also released discussion papers at the seminar. About 300 representatives, the majority of them women, discussed affirmative action issues related to the law, the media, public policy, funding, sponsorship, marketing, and education. It was evident from both the submissions to the committee and reactions during and after the seminar that there were conflicting discourses on how to address and redress access, opportunity, equity, and discrimination in sport (see Table 3.2).

One major discourse emphasized "playing by the rules," and was opposed to any affirmative action initiatives. Most of its proponents were conservative, misogynist, homophobic, and antifeminist men and women who claimed that affirmative action initiatives were being foisted on sport by radical feminists and lesbians. Affirmative action in sport was seen as yet another unnecessary and unwelcome intrusion by the state that should be resisted because it interfered with women's "natural" roles as mothers and wives in nuclear families. "Kingpins" and a few "queen bees" who had risen to the top, and consequently believed that sport was meritocratic, were

TABLE 3.2
Ideal-type Subdiscourses of Affirmative Action in Australian Sport

"Play by the Rules Discourse	*"Change the Rules" Discourse*	*"Change the Game" Discourse*
Articulated by an ensemble of misogynist, homo-phobic, and anti-feminist men and women:	Articulated by an ensemble of men and women supporting liberal feminism:	Articulated by an ensemble of women supporting radical pluralism
• Old girls • Old boys • Queen bees • Kingpins	• Essentialists • Pragmatists • Marketeers • Players • Spectators	

afraid that affirmative action policies would antagonize their male colleagues. "Old boys" and "old girls" maintained that affirmative action policies were tantamount to tokenism and reverse discrimination.

A second major discourse championed "changing the rules." Its supporters believed that affirmative action initiatives would dismantle the barriers that prevented women from competing on a "level playing field" with men. There were three variations of this liberal-feminist discourse. "Essentialists" argued that women were inherently more benevolent than men and would humanize sport once they entered it in greater numbers and rose to the top. "Pragmatists" asserted that numbers—not virtue—was what counted, and that it was vital simply to get "jobs for the girls." "Marketeers" maintained that women had to follow the example of "successful" male sports which had professionalized and glamorized their images in order to obtain a bigger slice of the sponsorship pie and more media coverage. This group deemed the "kitchen table" style of the "old girls" to be outmoded and pushed for the entry of experts skilled in marketing and management. Supporters of liberal-feminism were further divided into two other camps. On the one hand were "players"—athletes, coaches, and administrators seeking a better deal for women in their particular sport, but who had little or no commitment to broader issues of affirmative action or the women's movement. On the other hand were "spectators"—bureaucrats and politicians who had little or no personal involvement in sport, but saw it as an important arena into which affirmative action principles ought to be extended.

A third, and decidedly minor, discourse was articulated by a few lesbian and heterosexual women who focused on the desirability of "changing the game." They supported affirmative action policies provided they encompassed men and women of different sexual, class, age, ethnic, and racial backgrounds and did not replicate undesirable aspects of the hegemonic male model.

During the seminar, the ASC had been subjected to considerable criticism, with one keynote speaker noting that its own affirmative action policies were lacking. In his concluding comments, the executive director stated his intention to pursue affirmative action both within and outside the ASC. By the time the seminar concluded, liberal-feminism had clearly gained ascendancy, despite its internal divisions and opposition from other discourses.

It was obvious from the "Sportswomen Step Forward Conference," held jointly by the ASC and the New South Wales International Sporting Events Council in June 1991, that proponents of corporate feminism and enterprise culture had the commission's backing. In the foreword to the conference program, Ros Kelly, the federal minister for sport, noted that under the motto "Sport for all Australians," her government had "initiated a number of programs aimed at improving the participation and status of women in sport." She stated that sport needed more women administrators, coaches, and leaders, and that the purpose of the conference was to "increase women's confidence and develop their leadership and management skills" (ASC 1991b, i).

Now, there was little in the minister's comments to dis-agree with in principle—women *are* massively underrepre-sented in decision—making positions in Australian sport; some women *do* lack conviction about their ability to lead and man-age; and it *is* important to provide opportunities to increase women's access to decision-making positions. However, it is highly questionable to assume that "getting more women into sport" means that it is individual women who must change *their* behavior in order to compete more effectively in the corporate male arena. For it was made clear to the overwhelmingly female audience (in terms almost identical to the New Zealand situa-tion described earlier by Bell and Hayes) that the conference was explicitly designed to "package," "fix-up," and "fast track" *individual* women managers, rather than to develop strategies for how women might *collectively* challenge hegemonic mas-culinity in both management and sport. The following titles of some of the papers and workshops clearly illustrate the corpo-rate-managerial and individualistic tenor of the proceedings:

- Entrepreneurial Skills
- Determining Your Own Success
- Essence of Success: A Personal Perspective
- Time Management
- Decision-making
- Leadership
- Motivation
- Empowerment
- Perseverance
- Managing Self and People
- The Coach as an Entrepreneur and a Manager of People

Catherine De Vrye, a management development consul-tant for IBM, spoke on several of these topics by combining slo-gans from the Harvard Business School ("there are no prob-lems, only opportunities"; "with risk comes reward"), social Darwinism ("grow or die!"), and the locker room ("no pain, no gain!"). According to Leigh Maloney, whose topic was "packaging oneself," sportswomen had to present an "appropriate image" if they wanted to attract media coverage and sponsorship. Furthermore, she attributed the scant coverage of women's sport to the disinterest of women's magazines, and not to male sports journalists, who were genuinely interested in women's sport. This was a rather startling assertion, given the overwrought reactions by male sports journalists to affirmative action proposals that will be examined in chapter 6.

A few participants suggested that women could and should provide an alternative to the male model, but little time was allowed for dissident speakers. The dinner speech by renowned barrister and feminist Jocelynne Scutt, which actually dealt with flesh and blood women instead of "packages"—but hardly touched on sport—was deemed "too heavy" by many representatives. Others crowed that lesbians and feminist "ratbags" had been put in their place by the conference. During the restricted times for questions, several delegates tried to raise issues of lesbianism, homophobia, men's control of the mass media, and the structural nature of women's oppression in sport and society. In most cases, their queries were met with either "blame-the-victim" rhetoric or sporting cliches. For instance, one delegate declared her amazement at the supportive networks that most speakers enjoyed, and she asked what advice a panel of "queen bees" and a "kingpin" had for aboriginal, migrant, poor, or single parent women, who had neither the $250 registration fee for the conference nor the time and child care facilities to participate in sport. In a response that would have warmed the hearts of Nike executives, Commonwealth Games champion and Olympian Lisa Curry-Kenny replied, "just do it"! Curry-Kenny's ability to "just do it" rests largely on the fact that she has an estimated annual income of $250,000, a swimming coach, a strength and conditioning trainer, a full-time nanny and secretary, and a wealthy, supportive husband.

What was not on the 1991 conference agenda also was revealing. Speakers' depictions of the corporate world contained no references to monopolies, oligopolies, cartels, golden parachutes, phantom companies, inside trading, tax evasion, glass ceilings, old boys' networks, the double shift of paid and unpaid labor, or sexual harassment. There were no Alan Bonds or Gordon Gekkos. In fact, the "corporate Olympics" were portrayed as androgynous—even female-friendly. Several speakers stressed that although some men were resistant to having sportswomen in management positions, most were sympathetic and should be sought as mentors. "Be nice to men," "humor men," and "there's no need for confrontation" became some of the prominent buzz phrases of the conference. Apparently the only factor holding women back was their individual failings and desires, not the limited number of jobs available or men's control of sporting organizations.

To recap, we have a sporting version of the post-feminist myth that contemporary women can "have it all." But, like all myths, the sporting variant of the "new woman" naturalizes and depoliticizes power relations. The myth suggests that men and women live in gender-neutral societies that function as "naturally" as sporting contests between strong and weak, and between healthy and unhealthy competitors. However, this selective account of social reality does not address either the social inequalities of class, race, age, ethnicity, and disability (both among and between men and women) regarding access to sport, or the structures that deter girls and women in general from considering sport to be a desirable activity and deciding to get involved and stay involved in it for extended periods.

SUMMARY

In this chapter I have shown how the "corporate push" in Australian, Canadian, and New Zealand amateur sport has been facilitated by state doctrines of economic fundamentalism and corporate-managerialism. These policies have transformed the traditional financial infrastructure and grass roots bases, shifting most amateur sporting organizations from the "kitchen table" to the "boardroom" or "executive office" (see Table 3.3). I also have argued that affirmative action policies

TABLE 3.3
Institutionally Specific Design Archetypes for NSOs*

	Kitchen Table Type	Boardroom Type	Executive Office Type
Orientation	Private, volunteer, non-profit (membership and fund raising)	Private, volunteer, non-profit (public and private funds)	Private, volunteer, non-profit (government and corporate funds)
Domain	Broad: mass and high performance sport	Narrow: high performance sport	Narrow: high performance sport
Principles of Organizing	Minimal coordination; decision-making by volunteer executives	Volunteer hierarchy and professionally assisted	Formal planning; professionally led and volunteer assisted
Special-ization	Roles based on interest and loyalty	Specialized roles and committees	Professional, technical and administrative expertise
Standard-ization	Few rules; little planning	Formal roles, rules and programs	Formal roles, rules and programs
Central-ization	Decisions made by a few volunteers	Decisions made by a volunteer board	Decisions decentralized to a professional staff
Gender Regime	Controlled almost exclusively by "old boys"	Controlled by a mixture of "old boys," corporate men, and a few corporate women	Controlled by corporate men and a few corporate women

*Source: Adapted from L. Kikulius et al., "Institutionally Specific Design Archetypes: A Framework for Understanding Change in National Sport Organizations." *International Review for the Sociology of Sport* 27 (1992): 28–35.

in sport have been framed by a complex interplay of economic rationalism, neoliberalism, corporate-managerialism, corporate masculinity, and corporate feminism. A key question, then, is the extent to which affirmative action initiatives in sport can effect more equitable gender relations in an arena that valorizes elite performance so prominently and is so deeply embedded in the corporate-managerial state. I maintain that the intricate, discursive formations described above set resolute limits on how affirmative action can be "done" in sporting organizations, because women are framed as subject-citizens who can be successful, enterprising *individuals* provided that they compete on men's terms in a seemingly meritocratic system. I examine this issue in more detail in the next two chapters.

Four

Structures of
Labor, Power, and Cathexis

IN THE LAST CHAPTER I analyzed gender relations and identities at the relatively macro level of the state. I now adopt a more micro level perspective by examining men and women managers' perceptions of their organizational cultures.

METHODS

Between 1991 and 1994 I conducted in-depth interviews with men and women in middle and senior management positions in sporting organizations in Australia, Canada, and New Zealand. The project had the support of the ASC, SC, and the HC. In Canada, I interviewed seven men and eight women who were current or former managers in SC and two managers and four women members of CAAWS. In New Zealand, I interviewed four men and seven women who were current or former managers in the HC. In Australia, I conducted interviews with forty-six men and forty-five women who were current or former managers in all federal and regional departments responsible for affirmative action in sport, in a variety of organizations funded by federal and/or state authorities, and in organizations that were privately funded. A purposive sample was used in order to include voluntary and private bodies, federal and state departments, a wide array of sports, a broad range of managerial responsibilities, and as many women managers as possible (see Appendix 1). I have ensured that the quotes selected are proportionate to the number of respondents from each country.

Potential participants were sent a form letter, then were telephoned to ask if they would take part in the study. With one exception, everyone agreed to participate. All interviewees were sent a questionnaire (see Appendix 2) that was completed and returned by 87% of the Australian men, 96% of the Australian women, and all of the Canadian and New Zealand subjects.

Most of the questionnaire items were adapted from standardized questions used in previous sport-specific studies of barriers to women coaches and managers (Hall et al. 1989; White and Brackenridge 1985; White et al. 1991) and in an inquiry into the hurdles faced by women in the Canadian public service (Ministry of Supply and Services 1991). The latter project, which was designed, administered, and analyzed by Statistics Canada and consisted of a self-administered questionnaire survey of more than 12,000 men and women, is one of the most exhaustive studies ever done on perceptions of barriers to advancement in organizations. I also used questions and techniques that have been used in well-known academic and policy studies of gender and work organizations (Collinson and Knights 1990; Marshall 1984; Morgan 1986; Morrison et al. 1987; Reskin and Roos 1990). Thus, the information collected with the questionnaires was based on items that have proven to be valid, reliable, and objective with thousands of respondents in closely related studies of organizational cultures. Pretesting went smoothly, and none of the participants expressed difficulties in comprehending questions during the study. Each participant was interviewed for about an hour. All but two conversations were recorded on audio cassettes and then transcribed.

Most interviewees were in their thirties or forties, had completed tertiary degrees, defined themselves as middle class, and came from Protestant, Anglo backgrounds. There were two women of color, no men of color, and no people with disabilities in the sample. Nearly all of the men were married or in de facto relationships with dependent children. Just over half of these men's partners were in the labor force. About two-thirds of the women were married or in de facto relationships with dependent children. Nearly all of these women's partners were in the labor force. Just over 90% of the men and 60% of the women held senior management positions, while the rest of the respondents were middle managers.

One aim of the study was to replicate prior research in Britain, Canada, Scandinavia and the USA, which found that the key decision-making positions in sporting organizations were overwhelmingly controlled by men (Fasting 1987; Fasting and Sisjord 1986; Hall et al. 1989; 1990; Knoppers 1992; Raivio 1986; West and Brackenridge 1990; White and Brackenridge 1985; White et al. 1991; Whitson and Macintosh 1990). However, I wished to go beyond the distributional and categorical limitations of these studies by focusing on the intersubjective and relational aspects of gender in organizations (Hall 1996). Consequently, I emulated previous studies which foregrounded men's and women's "voices" rather than counting numbers, in order to provide in-depth analyses of the meanings respondents assigned to their everyday experiences of organizational life (Freeman 1990; Hall 1993; Pringle 1988; Roper 1994; Williams 1995). A statistical summary of responses to the closed-ended questions by the Australian respondents is contained in Appendix 3. The following topics in the transcripts were analyzed qualitatively:

- career paths and plans
- instances of sexual prejudice and discrimination
- what barriers, if any, were mentioned to women managers in sporting organizations
- suggestions for recruiting and retaining more women managers
- perceptions of affirmative action initiatives by federal and/or state agencies.

Although I asked respondents to focus on barriers to women's advancement, I was primarily interested in how perceptions of them were related to the *active* construction of gender differences in organizations (Acker 1992; Crompton and Le Feuvre 1992; Epstein 1992; Game and Pringle 1986; Hearn and Parkin 1987; Hearn et al. 1990; Padavic 1991; Williams 1995). I also attempted to avoid the methodological trap of using male managers as the norm by which women managers should be measured (Legge 1987; Marshall 1984).

> Men were much less talkative than women about perceived barriers, affirmative action policy, prejudice, and discrimination, and wrote fewer responses to open-ended questions. Consequently, less in-depth information was elicited from them on these topics. The study was not designed to reveal characteristics of individuals, but to examine the perceptions of men and women occupying powerful managerial positions in sporting organizations. For this reason, and to maintain confidentiality, I have used pseudonyms and disguised all organizations, except in chapter 7, where the ASC is specifically mentioned.

Using in-depth interviews involved certain trade-offs. I had the advantage of being a white, able-bodied, professional man who had played, coached, and administered sport. These credentials confirmed me as someone who was competent at sport, an important criterion in the eyes of most men and women in sporting organizations. Thus, I was able to establish rapport with both men and women and offset the fact that I was conducting research on a topic that is generally perceived to be a "woman's issue" and a "soft" area. However, it must be emphasized that in-depth interviewing always occurs in a gendered context, and men and women probably responded differently to my presence (McKeganey and Bloor 1991; Morgan 1981; Roper 1994; Williams and Heikes 1993). The use of in-depth interviews and open-ended items provided rich, qualitative data on respondents" *perceptions* of their work cultures. However, this advantage has to be weighed against the fact that both men and women tend to stereotype their own behavior to about the same extent that they stereotype that of others (Epstein 1991).

STRUCTURES OF LABOR

Women were acutely aware of what one of them jokingly called the "pecker order" in their organizations:

> The women are concentrated at the lower levels of responsibility and virtually non-existent at the top level of decision-making. If you were going to pick out a glass ceiling in this organization, it's at the middle management level. The sports science area is very much a male bastion in a sense in that it requires the technical expertise, and that particular definition of technical expertise often excludes a lot of women. (Gillian)

Gordon gave an example of how sports for people with disabilities were stereotyped on the basis of gender:

> In disabled sports we have the opposite problem of the "generic" sports. We're typical of most disabled organizations in that about 75% of our executive and board are women. We have no trouble attracting competent women. It would be tremendous to have more men around here but they don't see disabled sport as a very glamorous field. Mind you, some will use disabled sport as a stepping stone and then head for greener pastures. We badly need men here because the largest percentage of injuries we deal with involve men and a lot of these are a result of sporting activities. It has been my experience that men put us in the "caring" or "social work" category that women traditionally have done; they prefer to work in the "real" sports.

When asked why there were so few women in decision-making positions, men usually gave two types of responses. There were those who attributed women's underrepresentation to "tradition," "society," or "natural" sexual differences. For example, Jon attributed the low number of women managers in sport to the fact that "they're basically not tough enough. Maybe it's hormonal or something, because they crack under pressure a lot of the time." Other men saw gendered managerial structures as the outcome of meritocratic competition:

> I am aware that barriers may have been put in front of women in the past—their upbringing and things like that. We realize that we've got a problem and need to do a few things positively to make sure they have got the same opportunities as men to gain experience. But I really don't think when it comes to employment there's a problem. In my experience, it's always been based on whether the person could do the job or not. (Dick)

By contrast, women tended to perceive that men's strong networks and insensitivity to women's family commitments substantially disadvantaged their career prospects. The particularly masculine ambience of sport and the strength of sporting networks were often perceived to be formidable barriers for aspiring women managers:

> I just feel that around here you can be an incompetent male and just be called incompetent. If you're an incompetent female, you're really down the totem pole. It's the same as sport—"You are playing like a girl"—the ultimate put-down. (Jeanine)

> The old boy network really shuts them out. We have beer and pizza nights for volunteers and it's almost like the separate pubs and buildings they used to have for men only at one time. It's an attitude and ambience that seems to be male-dominated right now, and I think it takes a strong woman—an autocrat—to put up with that crap at the local level. *I* find it very hard. I think that's how most volunteers get involved at the local level, so women are really blocked there, especially when there's only one or two of them to begin with. (Gareth)

When you look at sport generally you're looking at *the* Australian ethos and culture. The major sports are all essentially male-dominated and they appeal to the male; they're part of the "macho" image. Guys play sport, but for many, many girls we know the problems—opting out of sport now by about age 14. It's not hip, it's not cool for girls to be playing sport. Women haven't gone through that phase where they've been involved with the sport ethos, except for netball, women's hockey, and a few other areas. I've been involved in some combined sports, but they were totally dominated by the men. So those guys who are experienced then become club officials and the women become scorers, secretaries, or whatever. Part of that is because the males just reckon they can basically do it better, even if it's unconscious. The people who have come up through the ranks in this organization are not much different. (Carl)

When I asked Grant if his background in sport helped him get on in the business world he replied:

Unquestionably! Sport, like alcohol, cuts across social boundaries and different cultures. I think it provides that sort of common linkage between different groups of people. In business, that old boys' network is very important. You get to size up people and know their capacities. Of course, networks aren't exclusive to sport, they're across all sectors of the society. I think it's a fair statement that women don't fit in comfortably or aren't invited comfortably into all-male, boys' own circles. (Grant)

I asked Kristin to elaborate on the "operational styles" of men and women managers:

Part of it is the way men relate to each other, especially in sport. It's a very strong sort of "buddy system," a strong sense of "mateship." I think it stems from the feeling that men get from being in the same sporting environment which makes them relate to each other in the same way in the workplace. Men will "groom" another man but a woman really doesn't belong in the scene, so she's not really the sort of person that's going to be groomed by the mentor. I just don't think that men perceive women as being in the same league. Women don't circulate in the mateship area. Women don't use the same rules or use the same change rooms. Lots of informal discussion goes on in those sorts of environments and women just aren't there. Developing networks for women is fairly new and I don't really know how effective it's going to be. The problem with women's networks is that they don't have the power brokers involved. A couple of mates high up will listen to a man. It doesn't really matter what their position in the hierarchy is, they'll listen to each other. If you're outside that network, and women are, then you have to convince people that the reason that you should be listened to is because you've got something good to say. So, you have to do the convincing first.

I asked Jeremy, a senior manager, if any men or women in his organization were capable of replacing his CEO:

I have no doubt that outside the organization there could be some women; internally, I would have to say, no. There definitely are men around here.

Q: What makes the men around here better candidates than the women?

A: Their extensive networks . . . things like going to conferences and being known by organizations without having to go out and solicit or being seen to be pushing your own barrow.

A few women used their sporting backgrounds to penetrate men's networks. One was Belinda, who had been an international calibre runner:

Who you run with at lunch time is the key, if you can get in the top running group. There is the A team—they actually call themselves the A team [laughs]—which is all guys except for me. Then there is the B team and the C team. For the boys, it's a matter of working your way up. Everyone knew about my [running] background, but I never got invited to run with the A team, so I just showed up one day and started running.

Q: What was their response?

A: Well, some of the guys were pretty good runners themselves and they were okay. But I could see that the guys who were ultra-competitive, but not all that great, weren't happy once they couldn't keep up with me. I mean, it was just a training run for me, and I felt like going for a serious run afterwards. I could have left them all for dead at any time, but I just coasted and finished with the frontrunners, because I wasn't out there to run; I was out there to network. I basically use it now for getting the gossip that I wouldn't get otherwise. As a woman, I'm naturally not invited into their clubs and pubs—so it's the only chance I have to access that all-male network.

Three women were taking golf lessons in order to break into or facilitate networks. Rachel, who had competed in sport at the international level, explained that she was taking lessons because:

I kept going to tournaments organized by our corporate sponsors, where I just sat by myself in the clubhouse and waited for the boys to come back from their round. So, I decided that if I was going to make full use of those networks, then I'd better get out there too.

Nina, an accomplished golfer, stated that the golf course was the place where she and her boss made most of the important decisions about their organization:

If he comes to see me late in the afternoon to see if I just want to play a couple of holes, I know he just wants to toss some ideas around. If he drops in before lunch wanting to play the back nine, then he's got something on his mind. If he wants to play 18 holes then I know it's got to be something really important.

Although women did not begrudge men having networks *per se*, they perceived that this gave them a built-in advantage for recruitment, hiring, training, and promotion:

The biggest disadvantage for women—it's particularly applicable in sport—is the "combing" process that goes on. A person in management or a senior person will be looking to other people in the organization that they feel are very similar in their style of operation, and they start grooming them to adopt the same management style or the same organizational style to follow in their footsteps. That doesn't happen with women because men in senior positions don't easily groom women. For a start, they're women, and I don't think they see them as having the same sort of managerial style. So, there are not too many women in senior management positions that might adopt a woman and start grooming them to take on greater responsibilities. (Greta)

Denise organized several nights for women managers to get together for a few drinks because:

. . . women don't have a support group—they're just sort of thrown into things. It was funny because they soon found out that they all had the same problems. But because they don't have much support, they didn't realize others were going through the same problems—like being left out of information on jobs coming up.

Michelle's comments illustrate the immense differences between the drinking networks of men and women:

The men here will go out at lunch time to the pub with the business community, also an all-male group, so the networking is fairly tight. The men have lunches once a month and the rest of the day is lost. They don't do any business after they have been to their luncheon because the booze just flows. I went once and would never go again because I could see no sense in anything that was done there—certainly not ingratiating myself to a sponsor by drinking him under the table! It's very hard for women to invite either a male or a female to a pub to do business. They certainly wouldn't get themselves inebriated to do so, so there's just no old girls' network.

None of the organizations had on-site child care centers, and most men viewed childcare as a "woman's issue." Irrespective of their marital status, nearly all men had continuous career paths and only one had taken paternity leave. Ben stated that he had experienced a "dream run" in his career:

I was able to get a lot of leave during a previous job. See, a guy is able to take punt and an opportunity. Psychologically, they're more inclined to say, "I will move from this stream to this stream." With women, many of them move up the ladder and take their time until they find a bottleneck. If they're satisfied or in a relationship, I believe many of them will stay in that position rather than move out. If I saw an opportunity, say in Melbourne, I would move and take my wife with me.

Although single women and married women without children tended to have continuous career paths, all married women's paths had been disrupted by marriage, childbirth, a partner's change in employment, or domestic responsibilities. Whereas married men could put paid work ahead of domestic responsibilities, most married women had to balance both spheres even when they had considerate partners. A typical example was Rose, a former Olympian with over ten years of managerial experience in several NSOs and a multinational company. Rose has crossed Australia twice as a result of her husband being transferred. She was attempting to have her part-time position (which actually takes up about forty hours a week) upgraded to a full-time one. Despite having a husband who is "unbelievably supportive," Rose's career has been severely affected by domestic responsibilities:

> The days have to start early—make breakfast . . . get the kids out the door to school . . . drop the youngest at preschool on the way here . . . get home and then get the children to swimming lessons . . . back home for tea . . . try to catch up on some work from the office and then maybe go out to an official function. I've tried to keep up my squash, but I've dropped a grade or two. Something that's gone by the way is my fitness.

I commented that her lifestyle sounded very hectic and stressful, to which she replied:

> It's always juggle and struggle. You have no choice except to be totally organized. You don't just get up and get dressed. You get the family fed and *then* you get dressed. Otherwise, you've got to wipe the vegemite and everything off you. At times it is difficult but I worked at being able to cope with it. At first I did secretarial and assistance work. I didn't take on anything in a totally responsible administration position because of the children. When I really look at it, I had a gap of probably eight years or so in my professional career.

Eleanor always tries to go to functions after work because:

> . . . it's really important for me to be there with the boys and have my section's point of view represented. But if I

was a single parent, even if I was really outgoing, it would be very difficult. I have a husband who's fantastic. He understands how important the after-work scene is for my career and can usually pick the kids up. I wouldn't say we split things 50/50, but the kids think he's the only one of us who can cook. I know I'm lucky because I see some of the other girls at work who don't get much help; they really struggle.

According to Faye:

It would be nice to have the luxury of some time to think about some issues like the men do. I would love to sit down outside of the real working hours with the men. Maybe not at the pub, but even over a few drinks here . . . just to float some issues which we tend not to get the time to do. But in order to do that there has to be a recognition on the part of men that in most cases, women have some family responsibilities, a whole area of responsibility that we have that makes it that much more difficult to perform.

Nicola stated that women's lives:

. . . tend to be very hectic, and it doesn't help when a meeting is scheduled during the "panic hours." That's around 8:30 in the morning when you've got kids to drop at school, so you have to make other arrangements. The worst time is from 5 to 5:30 p.m., especially if your husband can't get to child care before closing time. Meeting times here are set by the men, and we'd like to say, "Look we don't want any meetings before 9:00 a.m. or late afternoon because we've got children to attend to." I've dropped gentle hints about that but got vibes from them about maybe not having "commitment," so we tend not to say anything and make other arrangements. I wish they were more sensitive and would run with the government's policies on child care. You'd think they would be a bit sensitive because their wives drop them off every day, drop off the kids, pick them up, have tea ready when they get home. But maybe that's why they're not sensitive to it—they don't have to do it.

Women were generally unhappy and distressed about the inflexible schedules in their organizations:

I could be in here at 7:00 in the morning and be out by 3:00 and actually do my job a lot more effectively and efficiently, and still have quality time with my kids. But that goes right against the culture of this place, which ordains that you've got to be on deck—or *seen* to be here—while the midnight oil is burning. (Lynda)

Women without children repeatedly expressed amazement and admiration toward mothers. Katrina and her husband made a deliberate choice not to have children because:

I know I wouldn't have a hope of getting to the level where I intend going if we had them. Kids are the "kiss of death" for women around here who are ambitious. I know that I couldn't have got where I am if I had kids. I have to work twice as hard as blokes as it is. Women with children have to work ten times as hard as I do. I guess that's why the burn-out rate is so high, why they always look so tired and sick.

Marilyn stated that:

The worst case is X, whose husband drops her and the kids off in the morning. But he can't pick them up, so she gets them, takes them home, and gets the meal ready. As soon as [her husband] gets home, she comes back here and stays until eight or nine. She's told me that it's just so she can show the big boys that she's not a wimp, that she's prepared to put in the long hours.

As already noted, men were much less talkative than women about prejudice and discrimination. When I prompted men about how often they thought about gender-related issues, most indicated that they did so very rarely:

> Unless it comes up at times like right now, which is once in a blue moon, I can't say it's something that really comes to mind. (Dan)

> I sometimes catch myself when I've used "colorful" language that might be offensive to the ladies. But aside from that, I'd have to say that I don't pay much attention to relations between the sexes around here. (Calvin)

> I have to confess that working through your questionnaire was the first time I've really thought about it in any great detail. I suppose that a lot of what we do around here is related to the questions you asked, but I can't say it's something I lie awake at night contemplating. (Kevin)

Child care, travel, prolonged working hours, and domestic responsibilities had relatively little impact on married men's careers. Like married women, married men often mentioned that they had problems fulfilling both their work and family responsibilities. However, whereas most married men could separate their work and family duties and give priority to the former, most married women had to combine them. Women usually described this tension by using phrases like "struggle," "walking a tightrope," "double bind," "panic," "frantic," and "chaotic," whereas most men alluded to it in matter-of-fact ways:

> She's basically been supportive of my career moves and I've been of hers. She can do casual work. When we've moved she's always managed to pick up something, so that hasn't been a problem. (Ryan)

I asked Mike how he balanced work and family life:

I'm the gardener and the cook and the person that does all the creative housework. I cop-out by not doing the drudgery-type things. Cooking the exciting meals is something that's actually stimulating, so I do that. Mundane things like ironing and washing—things that have no mental stimulus—my wife does. I don't know if it's worked out that way from planning, but I certainly get the easy end of it because I get to do the more interesting things.

Q: Does your wife work?

A: Yes, she works 9 to 5. She's also the chauffeur for the kids—they are really into sport, and mum's the taxi.

Fred was able to combine a full-time professional job with a heavy administrative load in his sport:

At work I basically can bludge off my colleagues who cover for me and let me get on with doing administration. I know none of the women in the office could get away with that. Also, my wife has made the sacrifices and put up with the travel and hours and so on. The crunch will come if she decides that she wants to have a career, too.

Andrew stated that:

I do a lot of travel, and know my wife is the one always left at home looking after the kids when I go away. At the last minute I'll say, "I've got to fly off to Adelaide tomorrow," and just pack my bags and go. If the situation was reversed it would be very difficult, probably impossible, for one of us to look after the kids at the last minute like that.

The few men who dwelled on work/family tensions indicated that they felt guilty about being a "technically present but functionally absent father" (LaRossa 1995):

The day starts early with a jog when I make mental notes . . . back home where I jot down my thoughts from the run . . . at the desk by 7:30 . . . not home most nights until late . . . on the road a lot, too, away from the family.

Q: How do you balance your work and family life?

A: Well, I must say I have neglected the kids, and I'm not happy about that. As for my wife, I couldn't have got where I am without her support—she's been the back-stop. (Patrick)

It's a totally insane environment. You've got to make sure you're here early and don't leave before 6 p.m.—that's definitely not kosher. You've also got to come in on the weekends, at least for a while, just to be seen to be around. I just feel that things are measured more by the quantity than the quality of what you do. I'm not saying that our stuff is second-rate, but I could do the same amount of work in 10 or 12 hours over four days and then be able to spend some time with the kids. (Matt)

Outside work I'm also very involved in my sport. It makes me a very poor husband and father in terms of time. I still save face with the famous theory of quality time, but it's not quantity time, I'm afraid. I've found the workload here has increased tremendously over the years as we've downsized and people have not been replaced. My wife stays at home and she raises our kids. To some extent, that arrangement blunts a bit of the impact of my situation. She accepts . . . defines her job as keeping the home and being with the kids, so I think it's not as dramatic as if she were working outside, because obviously then she would expect me to do a hell of a lot more than I'm doing. But it's not a situation which I find right—I was going to say pleasant—but that's not exactly true. I mean, it's very pleasant for me because I like the work and I like being involved in my sport, but it's not right. (Tom)

These men surmised that although their situations were unsatisfactory, they were shrugged off as "the cost of being on top" (Patrick), the "total commitment demanded of everybody in the organization" (Tom), and the "price you pay if you want to move up the ranks" (Matt). Like most of the men in these "greedy institutions" (Coser 1974), their masculinity was validated by demonstrating that they could "put runs on the board" or "make the hard yards"—classic manifestations of the never-ending struggle of the "organization man" to prove and defend his masculinity (Collinson and Hearn 1994; Roper 1994; Winter and Robert 1980). Men's general unawareness of gender dynamics in their work and/or home settings exemplify Kimmel's concept of "invisible masculinity"—men's privileged position of being able to disregard the pervasiveness of gender and to think of themselves as genderless.

Managers can engender employee loyalty by formally acknowledging the gender imbalances in their organizations and ensuring that both men *and* women understand why they need to be redressed. The result is the creation of what Bennis (1990, 158) calls a *transitive* organization in which "job A prepares one for job B, which, in turn, prepares one for job C." Nearly all organizations in this study were *intransitive* in the eyes of most of the women, who felt that once they reached a certain level, either upward or even lateral movement was unlikely, if not impossible. When I asked participants if any model or combination of models in Table 4.1 resembled their organization, over 90 percent of the men believed that their organization corresponded to Model 4. Only about 10 percent of the women identified their organization as looking like this, and most reported intense feelings of exclusion and isolation. They used a variety of related metaphors to describe their situation: "glass ceilings," "brick walls," "hoops," "blockages," "hurdles," "ghettos," "on the outside looking in," "passing the ball but never having it passed back," "frozen out," "kept in the dark":

It's not the obvious stuff; it's the subtle physical barriers that men put up. If I go to a meeting with my boss and

TABLE 4.1
Structures of Hiring and Promotion By Gatekeepers
in Traditionally Male Organizations*

MODEL 1: "MEN ONLY": Sex is a *fundamental* consideration to gatekeepers. They hire and promote staff as qualified as possible, but will hire and promote unqualified men over highly qualified women.

Sex of Staff

Women	Women	Women		Men	Men	Men
Low	Moderate	High		Low	Moderate	High

Level of Qualification

MODEL 2: "MEN PREFERRED": Sex is a *moderate* consideration to gatekeepers. They prefer men, but will hire and promote very qualified women over unqualified men.

Sex of Staff

Women	Women	Men		Women	Men	Men
Low	Moderate	Low		High	Moderate	High

Level of Qualification

MODEL 3: "MEN GIVEN THE EDGE": Sex is a *minor* consideration to gatekeepers. They hire and promote the most qualified staff but, within levels of qualification, give men the edge over equally qualified women.

Sex of Staff

Women	Men	Women		Men	Women	Men
Low	Low	Moderate		Moderate	High	High

Level of Qualification

MODEL 4: "BEST PERSON FOR THE JOB": Sex is *irrelevant* to gatekeepers. They hire and promote the most qualified staff at all levels regardless of sex.

(continued on next page)

TABLE 4.1 *(continued from last page)*

Sex of Staff

Men and Women	Men and Women	Men and Women
Low	Moderate	High

Level of Qualification

Source: Adapted from B. Reskin and P. Roos, *Job Queues, Gender Queues: Women's Inroad Into Male Occupations* (Philadelphia: Temple University Press, 1990).

other males and have a slight difference of opinion with him, then there's a style of body language that he uses to basically put me in my place. So, at no stage am I ever allowed a forum where other people can possibly see my ideas and what I might have to contribute. Therefore, my ability to think issues through and demonstrate the fact that there's a workable solution are quite stifled by the way he treats me. For instance, at meetings he will lean forward, turn his shoulder away from me and address the men on the other side of the table. So every time I try to speak there is no eye contact and he speaks over the top of me. That is a classic behavior pattern. (Jacqui)

You might have talents, but the men don't know it because you don't get invited to drink with them or play sport with them and, of course, you don't use the urinal next to them. So, you don't get the chance to "advertise" yourself like they do. When men get to act up ten times in a row and you ask, "What's going on here, how come women never get a go?" the response is: "It's just the luck of the draw, it's got nothing to do with gender." So, you'd like to move into another area, especially when you know you're *at least* as good as they are based on how some of them perform—or don't perform. But you're frozen out, because that's not where women are supposed to belong. Some of the women call it a glass ceiling but it's a great big, bloody brick wall! (Lucy)

Like many other women, Cynthia cited instances of being treated as a "non-person":

> When you're the only woman at meetings or functions you sometimes feel there's this invisible wall between you and the men. I don't know how many of those situations I've been in when everybody has been introduced but me. At times like that it's hard to know what to do. The boss hasn't been polite enough to introduce you, but if you try to break in you can embarrass him and come across as a "pushy woman." Basically, it feels like you're being told, "You are not one of us." You feel really excluded.

Andrea has tried to break into the old boys' network because:

> . . . I've learned that's where a lot of the plotting and hatching goes on. But you have to draw the line somewhere. For instance, I won't go to a strip joint with the boys. I mean it's hardly conducive to talk about gender equity policy in a place like that!

Megan tried to sort out some problems with male executives on an overseas trip:

> They made some real stuff-ups administration-wise in public. I wasn't happy with them and neither were the players, and we wanted a meeting to sort things out. But they kept locking me out—literally! The men had meetings in their rooms so I couldn't be there. I mean, they wouldn't acknowledge me, they actively excluded me.

Several men and women alleged that they had witnessed cronyism in recruiting procedures. Many women gave examples of interviews that had been biased toward men:

> Some recent appointments have been a national scandal. It's been patronage—pure and simple—the fathers

anointing the sons. No female will ever get into a major position while that is allowed to happen. Women don't want "jobs for the girls"—our only chance is to try to win it on merit. But they have got to advertise the positions for that to happen. (Edwina)

I was acting in a position and was unsuccessful in getting the permanent position. The interview was a complete waste of time. It seemed to me that the panel was biased and trying to slaughter me. It appeared to me that a decision had already been made not to employ me. One of the other candidates rang me up and also expressed his concern at the behavior of the panel, so my assessment that the panel was biased was correct. Comments made to me by my colleagues indicated that nobody else in Australia had the credentials for the position. It turned out that they didn't want me or anybody from outside the boys' club. Finally, a decision was made to appoint an ex-footballer. He had extremely limited credentials and no experience in sports administration, but got the job. I got no feedback, and when I pressed the boss he avoided me. I hung in for a while then packed it in. (Heidi)

Anna indicated that she had been "naive" about the importance of men's networks until she sat on an interview panel:

Before that I thought it was just the "Hail fellow, well met" stuff. But I became aware that networks *really* made a difference. The bloke who is first up walks in the door and the chairman of the selection panel nearly breaks a leg jumping over the table getting to him. It's a poke in the arm and: "Gazza! Owyagoin, mate? Geez, haven't seen you since the last test at the SCG; Gazz, meet so an so." It was totally appalling! The guy was a real drongo, but there was no way *anybody* was going to get the job after that sort of positive treatment. All the assertiveness training courses in the world wouldn't have helped the women who were interviewed; they were down love-40 before they walked in the door. They didn't even follow the most basic guidelines for non-sexist interviews! At another interview I had to pull the chairman up afterwards because he asked one of the women what sports she liked—absolutely irrelevant to the job description!

Many women gave examples of having their careers blocked because of direct and indirect discrimination by male administrators:

> The women's subcommittee of [the organization's] world body asked me whether I would consider going on the board for the Pacific region. I said I would love to, but our president knocked it on the head. He said, "It's got to go here and it's got to go there and it will take too long." I said, "They have *invited* me, all I need is a letter from you saying you endorse my going on it." But no, he wouldn't do that. Then we got a new president of [the world body] and he said, "There are issues in the Pacific region that I'd like you to look into—get an endorsement from the Australian body." But this dickhead was still the president of the Australian body, so again, I couldn't get it and couldn't do anything about it. (Marianne)

Other women recounted feelings of frustration because their grievances had been dealt with unjustly. For instance, Lorraine complained that:

> These two blokes had really done the dirty on me. I tried to confront them several times, but they didn't have the guts to look me in the eye and kept avoiding me. So I lodged a formal grievance with the national executive. Would you believe that the board was all men, and two were the very ones I was addressing my criticism at? The hearing took place without me having any opportunity

69

to put my case or hear what they said! It is my belief that those guys actually said things, intentional or otherwise, that were not true and nobody could challenge it. I got a letter back ages later with a bit of an apology, saying that there was a bit of a misunderstanding—"Thank you for your comments, we are sorry this happened, bad luck." It was most unsatisfactory to say the least!

Angela expressed the sentiments of many women in describing what she thought was the "catch-22" situation in her organization:

> In one sense it *is* the best person for the job. The men here would *have* to say that or they'd be saying that they didn't deserve to be sitting in those chairs. But so many subtle hurdles get put in your way that, as a woman, you never get a chance to get into that inner circle where they select the boys for the top jobs. So, it's the best person for the job—but only for those who've been admitted to the inner sanctum to begin with.

STRUCTURES OF POWER

No men—but most women—indicated that they either had been sexually harassed or witnessed sexual harassment of other women. Two cases involved repeated acts of touching:

> One of my bosses would make comments and I would laugh them off and act like it was a joke. Then he would come and put his hand on me. I just didn't know how to handle him. I should have been able to say "You are a creep, don't do that!" But I couldn't. Part of that maybe is that girls aren't meant to make noises about it. (Barbara)

> I had one client who touched me three or four times. Finally, I just said, "I don't want you to touch me again,"

and he didn't. That's part of a whole syndrome, like the patronizing kind of "dear" and pats on the head and all that stuff that goes on around here. (Samantha)

Monica alleged that:

A friend of mine interviewed for a position and didn't get it. Her husband happened to be talking with somebody on the hiring committee who had loose lips and said that the reason she didn't get the job was because [a senior manager not on the selection committee] vetoed it. She was very distraught because this particular guy had made some advances towards her a year or so previously and she had rejected them. She felt it was purely based on that, because this guy has a reputation of being a sexual harasser.

One manager stated that her organization sacked a coach after he asked an adolescent athlete if she wanted to drink alcohol and try on some sweaters. A manager in another organization said that because of "sexual harassment of young women athletes by male coaches," her organization had instituted an "informal but firm policy" of sleeping arrangements on road trips.

The remaining cases were related to offensive jokes, insults, taunts, or innuendos:

There have been a number of coaching dinners where the after-dinner entertainment becomes a joke-telling session and the people in the audience are predominantly male. If you get six people sitting around a table and they start telling jokes, well, fine; but not, actually, as almost a formal part of the night's entertainment. The nature of most jokes, of course, are sexist. (Tanya)

I got up and walked out on a sports award dinner the other night. This guy was telling mother-in-law jokes.

They were really sexist, old jokes, and I just looked at my husband and said, "We don't have to sit here and listen to this crap do we?" He said, "No," so we got up and left. (Rachel)

I guess there are different definitions of harassment. We have had in the past, at the very senior level, examples of what I would call harassment—slaps on the bums, a chairman sticking his hand up a woman's dress, and things like that. I guess there's less of that really overt harassment now, but there are the jokes, more of a verbal sort of thing. And that does occur—*constantly*. (Sonia)

The put-down jokes that you have to put up with, the language, the barbs, and the jokes—over and over again—that wears pretty thin. That might be my impression of the level of sexual harassment—verbal harassment. [Men] think much of it's just for fun, but they don't realize by doing it all the time, it actually wears very thin and it's no longer fun, even though they see it still in that same light. It becomes offensive and doesn't assist the person working well on the job. (Nina)

The big power differential thing is always going down. Sexual harassment is basically a power thing—a male-female thing. But it's different when your client is [an NSO] and the CEO or board director comes on to you— that's a *really* big power thing that's difficult to deal with. It got to the point where a friend of mine punched one of those guys in the nose over it. (Gillian)

Researchers have identified myriad ways in which power and sexuality are structured in organizations. Morgan's (1986) cartography of heterosexual relationships in organizations underscores the point made in chapter 2 regarding the interplay of accommodation, acquiescence, and resistance involved in gender relations (see Table 4.2).

Men and women were very similar in perceiving that they possessed the personal abilities requisite for effective and efficient management (e.g., ambition, commitment, time-management skills, unafraid to take risks and make difficult decisions, capable of obtaining results). In describing their managerial styles, men displayed "paternalistic" and "corporate" masculinities (Collinson and Hearn 1994; Hearn 1994; Kanter 1977; McDowell and Court 1994; Roper 1994; Winter and Robert 1980). A paternalistic vocabulary was most common among men in later life, who used "gentlemanly," familial, and condescending terms to describe relations between men and women in their organizations. For instance, Lee explained that his NSO had no women on its board or as executives because:

> Basically, women just aren't interested in all the political bullshit that goes on around here. They just want to come and have a hit and stay out of all the kerfuffle that comes with administration.

Most of the younger men articulated aspects of corporate masculinity based on the contradictory motifs of competitive individualism and corporate loyalty (Kerfoot and Knights 1993), as well as elements of "rationality, calculation, and orderliness" (Connell 1990a, 521). These men depicted both their personal and organizational goals by using individualistic, combative, and sporting metaphors (e.g., "putting runs on the board," "making the hard yards," "leading from the front," "leading the troops," "putting the puck in the net," "slam-dunk," "scoring touchdowns"). When depicting successful leaders and organizations, these men regularly invoked archetypal male coaches, athletes, or teams, who were "tough," "determined," "well-coached," and "efficient." These two types of masculinities sometimes clashed, with young men claiming that older men's views about women impeded organizational efficiency and effectiveness. Eric, who was the national secretary of a sporting organization that he described as "more of a male

TABLE 4.2
Strategies Men and Women Use to "Manage" Gender Relations in Organizations*

Some Female Strategies		*Some Male Strategies*	
Queen Elizabeth I—	Rule with a firm hand, surrounding oneself as far as possible by submissive men. Margaret Thatcher provides a modern example.	The Warrior—	Frequently adopted by busy executives caught up in fighting corporate battles. Often used to bind women into roles as committed supporters.
The First Lady—	Be content to exercise power behind the throne, a tactic adopted by many "corporate wives" such as executive secretaries and special assistants.	The Father—	Often used to win the support of younger women searching for a mentor.
		King Henry VIII—	Use of absolute power to get what one wants, attracting and discarding female supporters according to their usefulness.
The Invisible Woman—	Adopt a low profile and try and blend with one's surroundings, exercising influence in whatever ways one can.		
The Great Mother—	Consolidate power through caring and nurturing.	The Playboy—	Use of sex appeal (both real and imagined) to win support and favor from female colleagues. Often adopted by executives lacking a more stable power base.

(continued on next page)

TABLE 4.2 *(continued from last page)*

Some Female Strategies		*Some Male Strategies*	
The Liberationist—	Play rough and give as good as you get; be outspoken and always make a stand in favor of the role of women.	The Jock—	Based on various kinds of "display behavior" concerned to attract and convince women of one's corporate prowess. Often used to develop admiration and support from women in subordinate or lateral positions.
The Amazon—	Be a leader of women. This style is especially successful when one can build a powerful coalition by placing like-minded women in influential positions.	The Little Boy—	Often used to try and "get one's way" in difficult situations, especially in relation to female coworkers and subordinates. The role may take many forms, e.g., the "angry little boy" who throws a temper to create a stir and force action; the "frustrated or whining little boy" who tries to cultivate sympathy; and the "cute little boy" who tries to curry favor, especially when he's in a jam.
Delilah—	Use the powers of seduction to win over key figures in male-dominated organizations.		
Joan of Arc—	Use the power of a shared cause and mission to transcend the fact that you are a woman, and gain widespread male support.	The Good Friend—	Often used to develop partnerships with female colleagues, either as confidants or as key sources of information and advice.
The Daughter—	Find a "father figure" prepared to act as a sponsor and mentor.	The Chauvinist Pig—	Often used by men who feel threatened by the presence of women. Characterized by use of various "degradation" rituals, which seek to undermine the status of women and their contributions.

Source: G. Morgan, *Images of Organizations* (New York: Sage, 1986). Reprinted with permission.

bastion than the army," indicated that he was being hampered by his executive and board members' traditional views about women:

> When what I call "the venerable gentlemen" meet, it's very, very difficult for me to make the administrative arrangements. I've often thought it would be good to have a secretary to do all of it for me, but they are really resistant to having a woman—any woman. I mean, it could be a male secretary—that'd be okay—but they couldn't have anybody hearing something she shouldn't or being offended by something she heard. I think there's just a sort of primeval resistance to having women intrude in the smoking room. We had a very important meeting here recently with [five international delegates] and one of them asked for an interpreter, who turned out to be a lady. The look of consternation on some of the old boys' faces when they saw that there was a lass in the room was a picture that would have been marvelous to snap. These guys have always dealt with committees of similar ilk, and the battleground antics of the boardroom can be a bit of a blood-bath. If you scour through the annual reports around the world, you certainly won't find any female committee members. The ladies have always cut the oranges and manned the canteen.

Eric also indicated that he was trying to "push for more women," because his sport's funding from the national agency was tied to its membership, and he was concerned that the organization was "losing girls to other traditionally macho sports":

> A few years back the gentlemen considered a recommendation by our coaching committee that we ought have a women's area, but it went into the "too hard" basket. But women have taken up [the sport] anyway, which has really shocked some of the old gin and tonic set. It's like,

"Goodness me, they actually play, you know!" And the fact that there was an international women's competition last year and or country wasn't represented has been a bit of an embarrassment. Some of these guys are actually thinking that maybe they really are a bit behind the times. I think that's been a catalyst for us to move, and we've caused some activity already. We are going to run a women's tournament over the next long weekend holiday, and we've applied to see if we can get some money from the [national agency] for it as a pilot scheme. That's a marvelous initiative which we have to support, if only because at least we are *seen* to be doing something. I am going to incorporate it into our next five-year plan and see what happens. I'm somewhat cynical about the elder statesmen, but I believe that it's well past time for us to do something in that direction. As I say, every boy who plays has a mother and a sister, and potentially they could be involved in some way.

Women also couched their personal and organizational aims in the conventional discourses of scientific management and corporate culture, but tended to complement these with concerns about means and ends related to equity, justice, and cooperation. Although women used sporting analogies too, they seldom nominated coaches, athletes, or teams to describe exemplary leaders and organizations. Women continually remarked that their consultative styles conflicted with men's adversarial tactics. According to Jenny:

Men judge it on male values; they look for someone who's going to be an aggressive and confrontationist table-thumper. When it comes to the crunch, that's what men around here want. They want to operate the system using that black and white, confrontationist approach, and I think that's why women get left out.

Laura did not apply for two executive positions:

I don't think my conciliatory style would have been taken seriously. As it turned out, the guys who got the jobs were "aggro," "macho" types—maybe that's why they were hired.

Two women related incidents with men that included physical intimidation. In Jane's case:

The guy just lost the plot. I mean the veins on his forehead were bulging . . . his fists were clenched and he was screaming right in my face. It was absolutely terrifying because no one had ever treated me like that, and I really was afraid he was going to hit me. He kept yelling things like, "You stupid woman! You idiot!" I had to tread *very* carefully after that and learned never to challenge a man in public again. I nearly quit the board, but thought, "Why should I let him bully me?"

It was clear that women who tried to be "one of the boys" in this masculine culture were in a "no-win" situation. Sean, who described himself as a "quiet achiever," indicated that:

There's no doubt it's more difficult for women to get into the workforce in a managerial area, and I think maybe the tendency that I have—sort of relatively low-key but still determined—isn't or may not be forceful enough for females. [Our chairman] is a fairly aggressive, dominating, controlling, assertive person. I think that would be far more difficult for a lot of people, a lot of the males to take, or to tolerate, if it came from a woman. It's more difficult for a "quiet achiever" female to get through the system, because it's necessary for them to be assertive and strong, to get through to dispel some of the stereotypes. But I think that can only get through to a certain level. To continue that assertiveness and try to break into the next level up may be more difficult for women. Men handle "aggro" better coming from a male than a female.

A female tyrant is probably much more difficult to tolerate than a male tyrant, for a male anyway, and probably
for a female, too.

Since most men believed that their organizations func-
tioned on the principle of equal opportunity, they generally
denied that they wielded power over women. Nigel, a NSO
manager, stated that:

I really think this affirmative action bandwagon has got-
ten out of hand. You can see for yourself that the girls
outnumber me around here—the receptionist and the secretary are both girls. We have a minister for sport who's a
woman and there are women's sports promotion units all
over the country. We're surrounded by women!

However, virtually all women perceived that men were
generally unwilling to recognize power differences and treat
them as equals. Consequently, women reported devoting considerable time and energy both resisting and accommodating
to their subordinate status:

There's a real dilemma in that we've formed an informal
group of women to try and deal with some of the issues.
We want to try and remain as private as possible because
we don't want to alienate ourselves as a group from the
guys. We could end up marginalizing ourselves if we don't
deal with it through the mainstream ways, and that's the
reason why we're trying to come up with some positive
strategies. Otherwise, we'll just get the same old, "Oh
here go that group of women again," which could have a
negative connotation in terms of what we're trying to do.
Their reaction is, "Why would a group of women want to
get together to discuss this?"—sort of a defensive mecha-
nism. I think women generally have a better understanding of equity and how you go about achieving it in
terms of special measures and so on than men do. I think

the majority of men still have a poor understanding of equity. So you walk a tightrope because in a good organization women should not have to be championing the causes of women. I guess we're a consciousness-raising and conscience-pricking group because we're not prepared to accept practices that we feel are just not fair. Our guess is that we will get strength from each other to articulate that better than if we were on our own. Collectively, we don't feel any ill-will towards most guys in this organization. They're pretty committed, good people to work with, but they just have a blind spot about women's issues. (Gwen)

Men just aren't aware of how subtle things are. They can't believe that they discriminate and they have no conception of what discrimination is. I don't think it's an intended thing. In fact, the biggest problem is that it is so subtle and so ingrained that they don't really understand how biased their thinking is. Unless you have good, smart women up there giving them a poke in the arm and saying, "Look, if that had been a bloke would you have acted that way?" then it'll never change. When you talk to them like that, some of them—the good ones—will take it in. There really is quite a change in their thinking—not as much as I would like—but it can change with some. The biggest thing is that we have to have change at the top. Whew! I know how hard that can be—it's an uphill struggle. (Melanie)

When asked if the examples of sexist behavior she mentioned were intentional, Lynda replied:

A: Oh, no! I'm positive it's completely unconscious. They've got no idea. Look, I actually like the guys, they're very nice people, not "macho" types, and the director has been very supportive up to a point. They just seem to think that women don't count—women are women and they're not part of the old boys' network. There's a kind of haze they get across their eyes whenever it comes to women's issues.

Q: Have you ever tried lifting the haze?

A: Yes, but how often do you have to do it—once a week? It's just such a huge barrier, but it never goes past, "Yes, we know that there are some problems that need looking into," and then down come the shutters again—they regress, they just can't see.

According to Georgina:

In the majority of sports it's not conscious discrimination. You have the dinosaurs who believe that women still belong in the kitchen or the bedroom, and they'll never change. You just have to wait for them to die off and hope that the more enlightened variety will replace them. In most cases I think it's just pure ignorance on the part of men.

Felicity wanted to believe that there were no barriers to women managers but was finding it increasingly difficult to sustain her conviction:

I like to think that it's not direct discrimination, that it's not because "She's a female." I challenged a case with the boss where I thought he was fast-tracking a relative newcomer. I pointed out that this guy would be getting a chance to pump up his c.v., and this would put him in a better position next time. The boss said that he just hadn't thought about it in those terms. I honestly think that is the problem most of the time. They're short-term fixes without any consideration of longer-term issues and the way they affect things. I don't know, it's really hard to know if you're disadvantaged because you don't drink with boys or because you don't go to the same golf course with them or because of other things. It's an intangible thing.

Although not one man perceived lack of self-confidence to be a limitation, nearly all women mentioned that it was an obstacle that they had to overcome. Whereas most men perceived that women in general lacked confidence, they were usually unable to explain why. However, most women and a few men saw confidence as part of a cycle of encouragement and opportunity. Jessica maintained that women tended not to apply for jobs because:

> They think: "Why bother, it's going to go to one of the old boys anyway." So you have to convince them that they're in there with a fair chance. They've *got* the ability, but often lack that important extra bit of confidence. That's why you need women at the higher level to ensure they are given the confidence that they can also get to that level.

Linda stated that she wasn't always confident:

> I am now, but it's something that had to be built. Doing an MBA was an eye-opener about men's abilities and lack of. I saw how men got to learn the business language that women don't get to use. I saw how they can transfer these skills to sport administration. Women often feel intimidated by what are very basic business terms. It's a bit ironic because women do most of the budgeting in the home.

Patricia reported that:

> Being a teacher helped my confidence, but I also saw fairly early in the piece that men could bluff their way through things. Without being aggressive I started to subtly pick them up on points. I know confidence is a big hurdle for women, but I always say to them, "Men overestimate their confidence and women underestimate theirs." Men get away with a lot by what I call "B & B"— bluffing and bullying. I guess you could say that men are confident, but I think a lot of that's because they're never

challenged by women. Women are *always* challenged by men, so as a woman, your confidence is constantly being undermined.

Bruce was one of the few men whose views were similar to women's:

I don't think men are prepared to take risks with women. They have got to do that because women haven't been tried and haven't been given the opportunities at the highest level. It's like picking a footy team full of blokes. Eventually you're going to say, "I have a feeling about that half back, or that five-eighth, or whatever. I think he's got the ability to do something, let's give him a try." The only way we're going to get women to go through is to take that risk. Women just haven't had the opportunities. They have had to drop out of their professional development and haven't had the chance to move into the networks.

According to Chase (1988), women in professional occupations have to contend with negative stereotypes about women in general. Time and again women complained that men held narrow, stereotypical views about their capabilities:

It takes people a little while to realize that being a female voice doesn't necessarily mean you're just the secretary and the kitchen table type. A lot of men still have the attitude, "Well, she'll go off in a few years and have some children," whereas they really should change their attitudes to say, "That's the person that suits the job, we must encourage her to stay." The male may stay for two years and think, "I've done as much as I can do and it's time to move on." (Belinda)

After I was hired I got to the first board meeting early. I had only met a couple of the board members and didn't know the bunch who rolled up first. One of them walked up to me and said, "How about getting us a cup of tea, love?" He assumed I was the bloody secretary there to serve him tea—never dreamed that *I* was the new manager! (June)

Because a lot of sports have come from the amateur background, women are still perceived as having that kitchen table mentality. Even though they might do all the invoices and accounts and everything at home, they are not thought of as having the capability of doing business—only men are business people. So women tend to get overlooked when it comes to the business side of sport. (Narelle)

There is the assumption that it would be awful to have a woman boss because old Fred Bloggs has been the president of the organization for a long time and he couldn't cope with this change—we had better not stir the pot too much. Men feel comfortable with male managers—that is the assumption—whereas a woman manager wouldn't "fit in." In terms of those positions, I think the unconscious assumption is that the job is beyond a woman's capability. There's also the assumption that it is not the right sort of work to offer a woman—"She won't be available to attend meetings because she has a family at home." So male-only experiences are the baseline for how their spouses or their mothers and girlfriends will operate. It gives them stereotypes of how other women will react and how capable they are of doing particular jobs. (April)

Some areas are seen to be suited for females and some for males. Sports development is very much the boys' network. Women in sports development tend to be in the "soft" or "easy" sports—gymnastics, etc. I get these messages that women aren't tough enough to handle "tough" sports, so men get to learn negotiation skills and women don't. I say, give us a chance to set up something with Rugby Union and Australian Rules and make us negotiate with men at that real, hard line. (Kylie)

Chase suggests that professional women try to dispel negative stereotypes by setting exceedingly high standards. This places women managers in a contradictory situation: they must perform extraordinarily well by men's criteria but in a manner that does not threaten men's stereotypes about "appropriate" feminine behavior; they need to be tough without being "macho"; to take risks, but also be consistently outstanding; to be ambitious, but not expect equal treatment; and to assume responsibility, but follow others' advice. Morrison et al. (1987, 60) liken this situation to that of a diving contest where "the dives performed by women must have a higher degree of difficulty, yet the judges do not follow the customary procedure of factoring the difficulty into the score they give."

Thus, Katrina's earlier statement that she felt she had to "work twice as hard as blokes" was reiterated by many other women:

We have to justify our point of view because men will *never* let you forget it if you slip up. We learn to pay attention to the finer points, whereas the boys can get away with some pretty vague stuff. I couldn't get away with— *no* woman could get away with—the quality of some of reports by men that have crossed my desk. (Marilyn)

Louise also had extremely high standards and made it clear that she did not want to be perceived as a *woman* manager, as this would discredit her. Like all women, she wanted to be judged on "merit" and not gender:

I don't fly the feminist flag, but I believe I'm doing my bit to advance women in sport. I have chosen to do that by not joining the feminist group because I want to be rec-

85

ognized for my individual talents, not because I rode on the coattails of some group—that would devalue my personal achievements.

None of the women, however, wanted to be become like men, that is, to be defemininized. For instance, many women used Margaret Thatcher as an example of an undesirable role model and were critical of powerful women who did not use their positions to assist other women:

> We've never really had a woman here who would stand up for women. There was one fairly powerful woman when we first started, but she was definitely a Queen Bee, who didn't help any other women. You'd have been better off having a bloke. (Monica)

> Unfortunately, there is a key woman on the board who doesn't understand gender equity—a kind of surrogate man. She's managed quite well in the situation, so she doesn't understand that there are barriers. (Cherie)

> There's a real need for feminists to be affirming other women, but not every woman is good at doing that. I've seen some pretty cutthroat women whose personal ambitions work against women in the organization. It's often the ones who get very threatened over other women who show skills and the potential to rise to an influential position. Some token women who are up there in the all-male world want it to stay that way. I think women at the top should be giving other women a leg up, not keeping them down. (Christine)

But in identifying themselves as professional women who wanted to be judged solely on merit, most women also distanced themselves from lesbianism and/or feminist practices that were outside a conventional liberal mode:

> I think there are a lot of women who just want to be referred to as a *female* than a feminist. I guess that's

because the tag often means a lesbian radical—short back
and sides. I prefer to be seen as someone who is very feminine. I don't want to get rid of guys; I think they are
great. I just want to change their attitudes. I think feminists create a picture of anti-men with women out in front
regardless of costs. That isn't what I want. I want us to
succeed because we have the talent and have contributions to make. While I appreciate that we need radicals to
create awareness in society, I think at the moment we
need the middle even more. (Edwina)

The word feminist is a bit of a problem because of the
perception of what is a feminist. To me, you don't have to
be very militant and aggressive. You can put women's
views in a rational way and discuss those without having
to have all the features of what I would call a feminist.
(Sarah)

In some ways I agree that we need a feminist perspective
here if it's a gentle approach to feminism. I think we've
made that start to happen here. At least there is a critical
mass of women around, and I give [the boss] credit for
listening to our views. When I say give him credit it
sounds awful . . . like we have to sort of bow and scrape to
get what you would consider to be normal recognition in
the organization. But I think some of the things that
we're asking for apply equally to males and females, and
if we had a better start for identifying personal needs or
career developments, then those situations might not
arise and everybody in the organization would feel as if
they're treated more equally. (Emma)

I'm not a feminist—I just want a fair-go for children, disabled sportspeople—whoever. I think there are a lot of
men who are discriminated against as well because they
are fat or wear glasses. The strong feminists to me are
Germaine Greer, the ones who appear so strong that they
are lesbians. I don't particularly care about that, but I

do believe that some of them go overboard and tend to be so one-tracked that they lose sight of all the factors surrounding decisions and that there are no grey areas— just black and white. They (feminists) can't differentiate between a "fair-go" and just making it open slather against men. (Rosalyn)

My definition of feminism is someone who tries to ensure that women get an equal go, so I guess I'm unashamedly a feminist. If I think that feminism is about taking a "big stick" approach to affirmative action, then I would probably shy from that because I simply believe that can ultimately have some negative effect. (Beth)

I'm not a feminist insofar as fairness is really what's most important to me, that in the end it's the best person for the job. I think some of the real feminists come across very aggressively and don't do our cause any good in the eyes of the male because it makes them very defensive. When they feel that their position is being threatened it just makes the next part of the progress a little bit more difficult. (Margaret)

Only four men stated that they had any sympathy for feminism, while the rest displayed attitudes of antagonism, bewilderment, and distaste. Many men caricatured feminism and/or simply equated it with lesbianism in an abject manner. Feminists were frequently accused of "having gone to far," being "male-bashers," and "destroying sport." The following exchange with Alf, one of the most powerful men in sport in his country, encapsulates these tendencies:

I'm highly critical of having separate forums for women's sport. The amount of time and money and manpower that goes into women's issues is just not right compared to other deficiencies in our sports system.

Q: What sorts of deficiencies?

A: Like improving the participation base in this country.

Q: Given that the base is smaller for women, what about the argument that it is smart management to implement special measures that will boost their numbers?

A: Well, I suppose there might be some logic in that, but what I want to know is what the promotion of women's sport does for sport itself. I think it splits off women's sport from the rest of sport and makes it a Trojan horse for the feminists.

A: In what way?

Q: Well, it's just another forum for the hairy-legged brigade.

Q: In what way?

A: I just think that the feminists shouldn't be infiltrating sport.

Q: You don't think that sport could benefit from a bit of feminist input?

A: No way! Look at the havoc they've wreaked everywhere else in society. I mean, just look at them—is that the way you'd want your daughter to dress? We can do quite nicely without that sort of element in sport, thank you.

STRUCTURES OF CATHEXIS

Not one man mentioned monitoring his bodily practices or personal appearance. However, many women commented that they regulated their everyday appearance in accordance with heterosexual taboos and in order to be taken seriously :

The guys can get up every morning and just grab the regulation white shirt and blue flannel suit out of the closet.

I have to stop and ask, "Who I am meeting with today?" If it's a board meeting, I have to put on a tweed jacket and long skirt because they're all old boys who are really conservative and used to the school marm. They'd freak right out if I ever walked in with a short skirt on. (Sonia)

I really like pastels, but never wear them because you don't want to be seen as a "girl." You never wear anything low-cut or see-through—that'd be seen as too sleazy. Anything frilly or lacy is out because you don't want to look like a bimbo. So you have to "power dress" if you want to be taken seriously—the ten-inch shoulder pads, the digital briefcase, the mobile phone [laughs]. (Kylie)

It's interesting how that old saying about double standards works on this floor. The guys walk around with their ties undone and shirtsleeves rolled up—kind of disheveled. If that was the women they'd be called frumps. So you always make sure that you look neat and professional. You wind up playing that "sugar and spice and all things nice" game. (Emma)

Such strategies of self-presentation were intertwined with the aforementioned dilemma of balancing professional and feminine identities. In the case of dress, most women engaged in desexualizing practices for two main reasons. First, they wanted to avoid having their professionalism discredited by innuendoes about "flaunting" their sexuality or "sleeping their way to the top"—tactics that both men and women were alleged to have used to undermine ambitious women. Second, they wanted to avoid any association with lesbianism.

Given the regime of heterosexism embedded in the structures of labor and power described above, it is not surprising that homosexuality had a deviant status. Some men and women expressed concern about the purportedly large number of lesbians in sport:

There's some sports out there where the women won't even look at a man. You've got to be worried about letting your daughter get involved in that sort of scene. (Alan)

The highlight of the year is our sportswomen's award dinner, when we invite the press and our sponsors. It's an occasion to present the acceptable face of women in sport, as opposed to the feminist presence, especially the lesbian influence, which isn't terribly appealing. (Marie)

My wife and I stopped our daughters from going to softball—it's just a haven for lesbians. It's like cycling—it used to be blokes on spokes; now it's all dykes on bikes [laughs]. (Angus)

Some men and women indicated that although they were "comfortable" with gays and lesbians, their coworkers, bosses, clients, and the general public were not:

Males tend to be concerned about the lesbian influence of women in sport more so than in other areas. They really make a big deal about it! They are more concerned about women's sexual influence than women are about gay guys, although there are plenty of gay guys in sport. Now I suspect maybe at least one in ten people in society might be homosexual, so the same figure would possibly apply around here. But the guys around here keep going on about how all the unmarried women in the office must be lesbians. (Madeleine)

I think sportsmen have a problem with gay women and a big problem with gay guys. [A former boss] had a policy of not employing gay women because he thought the [NSOs] couldn't handle it. (Beth)

There's a notion that some sports are dominated by lesbians, so the question that gets asked is: "How involved should [our organization] be in this and that sport?"

There's some folks that don't want their young girls being involved with the gays in the sport movement. (Frank)

There's probably some discomfort on the part of [the organizations] I liaise with. I've had some of them ask, "What's it like working for a dyke?" I don't think that's a fair question and I say, "Well, I don't think of my boss as a dyke. I think of her as my boss; she's leading the show here and doing a very good job of it." (Ross)

I've got a few friends around here who are closet gays. It would be very hard for them to come out because the boss would go off the wall—their careers would be over. (Jane)

Men feel safer talking to you if they can relate in a way that they understand—flirting or bantering—some traditional norms of behavior that allow them to relate to you. So if you're a feminist and you're in sport, then the men around here think you must be a lesbian and you want more power. It's like "Uh, I can't relate to you on any of these fronts." (Kristin)

Many women reported that because they played sport or were working in a traditionally male domain, they either had witnessed or been subjected to lesbian-baiting:

There is the perception that to play sport you must be a lesbian, especially if you are going to play for such a long period of time. If you don't end up marrying and decide to have a career, then you are changing the social stereotype. I guess people need a reason to explain all of that, so "lesbian" becomes a convenient label. (Dorothy)

We've got a really lovely young girl working for us, who's everything you would see in a mid-twenties, young, female blushing beauty. She's got a boyfriend, she goes out regularly with him in sporting crowds, and she often receives the comment, "So what's it like in the Lesbian Sports Promotion Unit?" It comes from people who should know better because they know all of the people that work here. It's a sort of put-down about the work they are doing. They may not be lesbian themselves, but they're standing up for lesbians, who are seen as a bit odd. To me, it's just another way of devaluing anything that women do. I suspect that maybe ten years ago I would have found lesbianism a bit of an oddity. But it doesn't really have an impact on me anymore at all. It's here, it's there, it's everywhere, it's a fact of life. But men—and I must say, a lot of women—just can't handle it. (Rebecca)

I think there is an underlying thinking within the sporting community that every woman in sport has to be a lesbian. I haven't seen any greater overproportion in sport than outside of sport. I think generally there is homophobia, and I think that sport is not exempt from that homophobia. In fact, because of the nature of sport, it's greater there than in any other institution. (Virginia)

Women who openly declared that they were feminists felt that heterosexual women's fear of being labeled lesbians and the conservative politics of sportswomen made it difficult to forge solidarity:

Women are afraid of being labelled with the "F" word—afraid they'll be looked upon as feminists. And there is also the "L" word. It's almost like, "Yeah, well, you're sporty so you've got to be radical and lesbian." The "F" and "L" words seem to go together—or so people think. I get those kinds of comments from [NSOs]. I don't know if it's a divide-and-rule thing, but many women here are terrified of being called a feminist because of its connotations. (Christine)

The problem with women in sport is that they don't understand what mainstream feminism is about—its diversity and understanding that I may be a lesbian and

93

you're a heterosexual, but we should get that out front, talk about it, and get on with getting on. It's no good hiding these differences. Women in sport are so conservative because they've bought right into the high performance model. They're cut off from grass roots recreation and grass roots feminism. Mainstream feminists see that what's going down in sport is the same as what's happening in other areas. But there also are the mainstream feminists who really don't see much point in dealing with sport because it isn't as important as abortion, reproduction, and so on. So sport tends to get colonized by fairly apolitical types of sportswomen . . . they identify first with being in sport and being a woman second. (Cherie)

Only one man indicated that he was gay:

I don't advertise the fact that I'm gay, but I don't hide it either. I guess I'm probably marked as gay because I prefer to do aerobics rather than hang out with the jogging and drinking crowd around here. I guess that would make me a bit suspect in itself. I think that as long as I'm happy to stay put at this level, it won't be a big issue. But the crunch may come if I decide to move up the ranks. Then I suspect that I may wind up like women who hit that glass ceiling. (Ron)

SUMMARY

The days of the male breadwinner-female housewife system of family life have gone. Yet this model still lies behind our work structures and lurks in the mind of the man in the gray flannel suit.

—Edgar 1991, v

In this chapter I have analyzed gendered structures of labor, power, and cathexis in sporting organizations. With respect to labor, most organizations were horizontally and vertically segregated on the basis of sex, and most women felt devalued, isolated, and excluded. Men were generally unaware of how women might be disadvantaged by policies related to child care, inflexible working hours, and masculine biases in recruiting, interviewing, hiring, training, and promotion. In most organizations, criteria like skill, merit, performance, and commitment were governed by the rules of married men with wives who stayed at home to raise children and do unpaid domestic labor. Regarding power, most women did not want to be defeminized by emulating men's combative managerial styles; but they also wanted to be judged on merit, and distanced themselves from being associated with lesbianism and any feminist practices that were not within a liberal framework. Many women indicated that they either had been harassed or witnessed varying kinds of harassment of other women in the workplace. In terms of cathexis, homosexuality had a transgressive status and homophobia was common. Probably the most telling indicator of women's subordinate status was that although some individual women managers held powerful positions, this usually entailed supervising other women in peripheral areas. Unlike men, women seldom had collective power, especially *over* men.

Five

"Doing" Affirmative Action

AN IMPORTANT ISSUE surrounding the implementation of affirmative action is the everyday meanings that people attach to it. In this chapter I reveal some of the contradictory and conflicting ways in which affirmative action was defined and deployed by men and women managers.

AFFIRMATIVE ACTION OPPONENTS

Although some men have welcomed women's entry into work organizations, analysts have documented widespread paternalism, flight, resistance, harassment, and misogyny (Cockburn 1991; Davidson and Cooper 1992, 1994; Reskin and Roos 1990). Like respondents to the Canadian study by Hall et al. (1989), some interviewees were antagonistic toward affirmative action because they believed that their organizations already were based on the principle of equal opportunity:

> We don't care around here if someone is a disabled black lesbian as long as they can do the job. (Mitch)

> When I stretch my mind, I can't honestly recall any situations that I've been involved in where women have been disadvantaged or men have been favored over women for any reason. I know it's talked about a lot around here, but I can't say that I've experienced it. (Keith)

> Maybe in the past there were obstacles, but not today. Women have moved in everywhere—Parliament, busi-

ness, etc. They practically run education! Women can do it if they really want to; it's a matter of putting their mind to it. (Marie)

It was often stated that qualified women could never be located and/or never expressed any interest in administrative positions. Consequently, even when all of the senior managers and/or board members in an organization were able-bodied white men, it was perceived that the best people were hired simply because there was a smaller pool of women to draw from. Few managers saw the need to include affirmative action in their strategic plans, and those who did only paid lip service to it:

It's basically a low priority. Right now, the main issues around here are getting and holding a job. (Nathan)

When I asked an NSO manager if affirmative action could be a useful way to recruit and retain women, he replied:

Well, it might help some sports, but not in any big way. We've probably reached the peak level of women at the top positions in sport right around the country. All this affirmative action stuff won't make any difference because of one indisputable fact—only women can have babies. So, they will always be handicapped unless men start having them. (Nick)

Other participants used a "pipeline" theory (Sinclair 1994) to oppose affirmative action, insisting that the traditionally low number of women at the top would increase when a sufficient quantity of women currently at the middle management level finally "broke through":

It's probably time-lag—a generational thing. Women are just starting to catch up with men in society, and I'm sure the same thing will be true in sport eventually. You can't

turn around in one fell swoop a couple of thousand years
of men having had their hands on all the levers. Rome
wasn't built in a day, you know. (Larry)

A few managers were overtly antagonistic to me because
I was studying affirmative action. After sending a form letter
to Reg, I telephoned to inquire about conducting an interview.
He indicated this would be unnecessary, as he could explain
his organization's attitude toward women managers very suc-
cinctly: "We don't hire them." When he did consent to be interviewed, Reg made it quite clear that the appropriate roles for
women in his paternalistic organization were playing "lady-
like" sports, acting as club secretaries, selling raffle tickets,
and making sandwiches and tea.

When I initially met one manager to arrange an interview, he invited me to retire to the far end of his office so I
would have a long enough run to hurdle the "mountain of rubbish" that had been published on women's sport over the past
few years. When I showed up for the interview a few days
later, his secretary ushered me into a boardroom where the
offending documents had been strategically arranged in the
middle of a large table. His assistant, whom I suspect may
have been sent in to soften me up, quickly expressed her dis-
pleasure by inquiring why I was "wasting yet more money on
useless information about women's sport." When her boss
eventually arrived, both of them harangued me about how "all
this feminist nonsense" was "destroying Australian sport."

AFFIRMATIVE ACTION SKEPTICS AND CYNICS

Many managers indicated that they were skeptical or cynical
about affirmative action because they perceived a double stan-
dard existed with respect to inaction by the government or
elected officials:

Look! If I saw something besides glossy publications and
conferences I'd be more impressed. But it's an absolute

joke for the [government] and [minister for sport] to be shoving gender equity down our throats. They are supposed to lead from the front, but look at the place; it's chock-a-block full of men . . . tell *them* to get their own house in order first before *they* start preaching to everybody else! (Trevor)

Some managers enunciated cynical views about affirmative action. For instance, Veronica observed that:

If the [government] were to dangle some carrots or money as an incentive, I suppose I could come up with some statements about setting goals or targets. A good manager can make it look like you've got a policy on anything. I just wrote a policy piece for the minister last week so he could have something to say at a media function. He and his minder were happy as can be about it. Of course, we have no intention of implementing it. So, we would have no problem in writing something that *looks* like we have an affirmative action policy. It's a different proposition if the [government] wants to get heavy and use "big stick" and "big sister" tactics. I doubt they'd do it because they know the general sport community probably wouldn't wear it. Anyway, it could prove awfully embarrassing for them when you consider they're top-heavy with blokes themselves. But if they threatened to tie it to funding, we'd probably have no choice but to comply.

Q: So you wouldn't initiate policies?

A: No, there would have to be some carrots or a gun at our head.

Opponents, skeptics, and cynics made a sharp distinction between "soft" (targets) and "hard" (quotas) versions of affirmative action. The latter option was dismissed outright by everyone, and the former approach was only perceived to be legitimate provided it did not threaten existing arrangements:

I think we've got to make sure we look a bit more broadly for our positions. But we want to make sure that we don't wind up going the other way and end up with quotas or reverse discrimination. That won't do women any good at all. (Jackson)

AFFIRMATIVE ACTION ADVOCATES

Some men stated that they favored affirmative action. David was supportive because of the nurturing qualities that he thought women brought to sport:

> We need to get more women because of that caregiving aspect they bring. It's been my experience with [NSOs] that the needs of youngsters seem to be addressed more by women. Like at last weekend's soccer tournament, the mothers were the first to embrace the youngsters off the field and cool them down. The fathers are more stand-offish and "macho."

Ian supported affirmative action because of its long-term payoffs in human resource management:

> I'd say that all things being equal, I'd take the woman on. Even if I was just a little concerned that the woman might be marginally less skillful, I'd take her on because it's an investment. Having a flat management structure here means that there's no room for promotion, so I have to ensure that people here have got the ability to go on to something better when they leave. Our Board would never wear quotas, so I change them by a philosophy of encouragement and subversion. I don't know how professional that is, but that's how I have to do it. Quotas only cause more antagonism by virtue of being seen as compulsory—strong arm tactics by "big brother."

Two men were sympathetic because their partners had experienced difficulty in returning to work:

> It's tough for women who have kids and are out of the workforce for a while and then try to get back in—even at a lower level. Therefore, interviewing committees have got to make sure that women who want to get back in have the opportunity to demonstrate that they're capable. That doesn't mean they'll win all the time, just that they'll be given an equal chance. That's how I understand equity. (Tony)

Three men indicated that their initial indifference to affirmative action had been changed as the result of interactions with an affirmative action manager:

> I wouldn't suggest that I'm a zealot on behalf of the women's movement, but I've been sensitized to the issues internally around here and understand that it's very important to take a look at it. [The affirmative action manager] gave me some interesting research on the needs of young girl athletes as compared to young boys, like the different tactics and strategies that coaches should use. So, I've been sensitized to that sort of stuff—for reflection. (Stan)

Two men stated that they had become supporters of affirmative action as a result of becoming aware of discrimination against their partners or daughters:

> I've sort of had it beaten it in to me [laughs] by [the affirmative action manager and her predecessor] who propagandized me about how guys like me are really important in working for equity because my three girls are into sport in a big way. It's true—it's something I didn't twig to before, but now I see how the girls always get treated like kind of second-class citizens. (Henry)

Two other exponents either had worked for women or had previous experience with affirmative action programs:

> A lot of blokes find it really hard to have a female boss. Having been a teacher, I got used to working with women pretty quickly. I had several female principals who were extremely competent, very efficient. Maybe some day blokes in sport will accept having women like that. But don't hold your breath. (Don)

> This affirmative action stuff is déjà vu for me. About ten years ago the company I was with realized it was missing out on a huge pool of resources. I hear the same red herrings now: "Women don't come forward" or "We can't find them, etc., etc." Guys find it hard to accept that the barriers women face are artificial, that they're *man*-made. (Albert)

Most women expressed ambivalent or qualified support for affirmative action, believing that it was undesirable but required, given that so many men were insensitive to gender inequalities:

> A lot of men have a hard time even accepting we can stand *beside* them. If men would change their attitude, then we wouldn't need affirmative action. But until that happens it's a "necessary evil." Even then you can't win because they throw it back at you by saying, "You're just pushing your own barrow." I say, "Well, men have been pushing their own barrows for centuries. Who's going to push women's barrows—men?" (Virginia)

> [Affirmative action] doesn't work because men say the right words out of fear of saying the wrong words. But that does not actually lead to them internalizing the issues and changing their practices. People are very good at saying the right things but without actually changing a thing. I'd much rather say that what we're trying to do is

work as a group of people, for people to come and change their behavior because it's something that they want to do or that they feel that they have a responsibility to do. I'd rather they change some small things and not feel guilty or threatened about it. I admire the hardline feminists tremendously because they've put themselves out on a limb and changed awareness radically. But I think the pendulum has swung back and now people are saying about affirmative action, "We agree—can you help us? How do we do it?" That means they've internalized the fact that they need to do something, and the question now is: How we can to work together? Some feminists say that 50 percent of everybody and everything has to be equal. But that way, you're only rewarding people for short-term stakes and setting them up for failure. I prefer to get them to look for measurable improvements. That means you're constantly rewarding people, so they start to feel more comfortable and less threatened and are more likely to take bigger and bigger steps. (Margaret)

I think the dilemma that the organization is in is that it's not very clear in terms of its guidelines. They don't have a philosophy in terms of practices and procedures; no directives—it just seems to happen. The situation is unclear, and that makes it frustrating because you don't understand the reasons and then you start to question your own position within the organization. You think, "Hang on, I've been in this organization for X years, as opposed to this guy who's just arrived on the scene but has been given the inside track. What's the story?" This starts to sow seeds of discontent in the sense that you're saying, "Someone is getting favorable treatment or someone is being fast-tracked." At a time when the organization *says* it's concerned about the lack of women in senior positions, it becomes even harder to comprehend. (Roberta)

Most of the men around here have learned to *say* the right things, to spout all the rhetoric about affirmative action. I've heard the boss parrot it in public dozens of times. It's the old, "Our organization is committed to ensuring that women have equal access and opportunity in sport . . . blah, blah, blah." But he never *does* anything about it . . . it's just a platitude. The guys here use sporting banter all the time—"win-win results," "a fair-go," "the level playing field," etc.—but they don't *practice* it. The problems are right in front of their faces, but after you raise it beyond a certain number of times you sort of hit this wall of, "Christ, here we go again with this feminist claptrap." End of story. (Rhonda)

One woman became an affirmative action supporter after her boss allegedly refused to ratify her promotion to a senior position:

I really felt that I was being badly treated and said I wanted a decision in twenty-four hours or I would commence legal action. Suddenly, because I was in a position where legal action was a threat, it was amazing how they reversed rudder. Up until that stage I had not taken much interest in the legislation, but I suddenly appreciated being in the position of having some back-up. That really alerted me to how territorial the boys were at the top. I became aware how entrenched their attitudes were . . . that they didn't take risks with females. Their attitude is "Yeah, end of the queue, back of the bus, wait your turn. If we *have* to accommodate you, well, that's where you'll have to sit." (Erica)

Not surprisingly, most of the robust supporters were affirmative action managers and/or women involved in sportswomen's advocacy organizations. In most cases these women's strong endorsement of affirmative action stemmed from direct contact with a feminist or a feminist organization that had politicized them (only three women in the study had any involvement with mainstream feminist politics). These women saw affirmative action as a step toward a larger project of reconfiguring sport in ways that valued women's experiences and dismantled competition, hierarchy, and aggression.

Nearly all affirmative action managers displayed an array of contradictory emotions associated with their work: idealism, pragmatism, disillusionment, demoralization, beleagueredness, and burn-out. Both Denise and Katrina believed that although affirmative action had been a qualified success, women needed to constitute a critical mass in sport:

> Having a woman at the top isn't enough. Many women have been in a situation like I used to be—the only woman on an international committee and being 100 percent totally ignored and excluded. After a while it gets to the stage where you say, "Well, I've got more interesting things to do with my life than be put in an incredibly difficult situation where I am ignored, or patronized, or harassed. I don't need this." So you opt out, and that is what I believe happens to many, many women in those cases. So, in order for us to be successful at getting women at all sorts of levels, we have to help them along. If you had, say, two women on a committee, at least you'd have someone there to share those incredibly negative experiences. (Denise)

> Visibility is really critical. If decisions are going to be made that reflect the interests of women, then women need to be at the table making those decisions. In the past, there hasn't been a significant enough number of women at the table. There's been a token woman or two, who've either felt they've lost their voice because to express and articulate the women's position was such a negative experience for them that they were co-opted and became honorary men. Or they did express a women's position and were disenfranchised. So they found the experience to be so negative that either they left on their own, saying "I don't need this, I'm busy enough with my

own commitments in life," or they were voted out. So I think it's really critical that we reach the 30 to 40 percent threshold so that the experience is a positive experience for women because so often it's been a really, really negative one. (Katrina)

Jacqui stated that managing affirmative action was a case of "the three U's: undervalued, undermined, and underpaid," and she needed to be pragmatic in her strategies:

Ideally, you want people to pursue [affirmative action] because they have internalized it as a core value and their attitudes have changed. However, I am satisfied if they simply change their behavior in order that sport is more accessible for girls and women. Hopefully, their attitudes may change afterwards. I've tried for years to change attitudes and not met with much success. So I've said, "Fine, we're out of the attitude-changing business. I want you to change your behavior, and here's how you can do it. What I want you to do differently as a coach is change your behavior in such and such a way." That's going to keep me satisfied for now. Granted, it isn't as powerful as the attitude shift, but short of generational change, I don't know how I change somebody's attitudes who hasn't bought into the core values of equity.

Similarly, Cynthia stated that she had:

. . . a bunch of different strategies, sort of hedging my bets, because change is really complex and you just never know what the likelihood of success is with any particular initiative. There have been some very successful things that I would never, ever have predicted and sure bets that just fell flat. As a result, I've spread strategies around. [The organization] has some men strategically placed on boards who are respected in the sport community. They speak on behalf of equity, and we're trying to get a men's network established because there are a lot of new age, gender-sensitive kind of guys out there who want to do something, who are kind of embarrassed at being a white, able-bodied male. They are caring, concerned guys who want to build a better future for their daughters, so that is a really powerful strategy, too. Often, when men speak they can say the same thing as a woman, but it has a different credibility factor. They can help us move the issue forward.

Every affirmative action manager said that the concept could not be "sold" on its own merits, but had to be tied to some kind of "carrot" or "stick":

I sell equity to men based on a very bottom-line business model because that's the argument I hear from them all the time. My response is, "Okay, let's look at this from a financial perspective. There's a lot of things you can do about equity that don't cost you a cent, and there's a lot of things that if you're real serious about can make a you a lot of money by making your sport more attractive to 52 percent of the population. Smart marketeers do it. The National Rifle Association in the United States is on a major marketing drive with products preying on women's fear of violence to tap into that market share [grimaces]. So why don't we tap into that huge pool of women too?" So my argument from the monetary side is that it's just good management. It's also the law, so if you're not equitable, you're opening yourself up to some legal challenges, which could cost you a whole lot of money. So, I tell them that they can do some things for free, they can make some money, and if they don't do it they can find themselves dishing out a lot of dough to lawyers. (Monica)

Megan and Ilene were frustrated at being labeled as managers of a "soft" area:

If it's equity or special populations, etc., you're perceived to be in a "fringe" area rather than in the "serious" sections like the corporate stuff. You can express an interest in those areas, but you'll never get a go because only the boys are seen as capable of handling it. (Megan)

It really makes me laugh when you indicate to men that there are no women in the top positions—not just here, but right around the country. You wouldn't believe what they say—things like, "Ah, what about women's sport— the petticoat mafia—why don't you have any men there?" Or, "Where is the Men's Sports Promotion Unit?" It is the most convoluted logic I've ever heard! Here we are getting knocked back time after time for the opportunity to get multiskilling and these guys say they can't get into the gender equity area! Not one of them has ever shown the remotest interest in it—they spend most of their time bagging it. It would be wonderful if just one of them expressed a *genuine* interest in it. But as things stand, any guy who expressed an interest in transferring out of one of the "real" sections across to equity or justice would be seen by his mates to be lowering his standards—you know, "That's women's work!" (Ilene)

Laura, Gwen, and Felicity articulated a common complaint that senior managers' failure to fund affirmative action adequately sent a contradictory message both internally and externally:

Money talks, so if the [government] comes out and says, "Okay, we really want more women coaches and we're prepared to fund it properly," then people are going to take notice. What I have to fight against is the [government] saying that it wants to increase women's participation, but not giving me the money to do it. That sends out the wrong signals to [NSOs]. So when I go out there to

109

talk to them about their gender equity plans, they just laugh at me and say, "Why doesn't the [government] put its money where its mouth is?" (Laura)

[Affirmative action] is really hard to sell to clients when they see how [the government] has cut its own program to the bone and at the same time is spending a lot of its cash chasing gold medals. (Gwen)

I would say that [affirmative action] is being acted upon *generally*—statements about having more women coaches, encouraging girls to participate more, etc.—there's been some money going to that. But let's walk the walk and talk the talk! Look at the funds we get compared to anti-doping. And why in heaven's name are we funding men's water polo at the Olympics when no competition is allowed for women's teams? We just get these little crumbs tossed to us and [the minister for sport] telling us we're doing a good job. Well, I love to hear that, but get out your check book. That's more meaningful to me than little platitudes. I mean we're talking about over 50 percent of the population here! (Felicity)

Melanie and Barbara felt disheartened by senior management's failure to impose sanctions on NSOs that did not meet affirmative action regulations:

In theory, we're supposed to come down on sports that don't comply with the guidelines by withdrawing their funds, but I could never imagine [the boss] doing that. We can tell organization X that we can help them do such and such about its dreadful record on women, but there is no way of forcing them to come to the party, no accountability, and no political will to do anything about it. So when a sport tells you to get stuffed, you can't do a damn thing about it. Your professional credibility is absolutely zero in a situation like that. (Melanie)

It's a constant battle with [NSOs]. They don't have a clue what gender equity is about—not even the basics. They know that they're supposed to include equity in their strategic plans, but it's a real struggle getting them to do even that. And those are the *good* ones. The rest could care less about the issue. It's not much better around here. A couple of men on the executive (board) have a rough idea of what equity is about, but the chairman doesn't. Nothing I've seen him do would indicate that it's even close to the back of his mind. The NSOs know it too, so they know can get away with blue murder. (Barbara)

Tanya felt weary from continuously having to "put out fires":

I worked really hard to get homophobia on the agenda, just to let parents know that they don't have to worry about their daughters being molested by lesbians when they play sport. Then the media got hold of our policy statement and said we were running an all-lesbian organization at the taxpayers' expense. It's a touchy subject at the best of times without having to deal with that kind of shit.

April was aggravated by always having to justify her program's existence to her co-workers:

It's a catch-22 isn't it? Men say it is hard to get women who've got the skills. But when you try to do something that would attract more women or broaden the field, you're told, "Oh, this is tokenism, it's reverse discrimination." Meanwhile, there are departments around this country full of football and racing types because a mate, often a minister, gave jobs to the boys. (Sharyn)

Three women who had been involved in affirmative action both as athletes and administrators despaired over the slow pace of change:

Some things have obviously changed for the better, but I honestly believe that we've just scratched the surface, because most sports are still dominated by men. Now we're getting this backlash just because a few scraps have been tossed our way. (Linda)

There've been some changes, but in science and technical areas—with the possible exception of physiotherapists—it's really been incredibly slow progress. For whatever reasons, certain kinds of occupations or activities in sport seem to be pretty heavily insulated from social trends in favor of more gender equity. If you don't push in those areas that seem to be able to withstand the gender equity tide, nothing's ever going to change, because there's incredible resistance to change already . . . whatever's going around in society, sport tends to be on the more conservative side of it, more to the right. (Patricia)

There have been some minor concessions, but we've had to fight for them every inch of the way. But it's still like swimming lessons. The boys are put in the shallow end with life preservers to paddle around. Then their coach says, "Well done! My, aren't we good boys?" Meanwhile, a woman gets tossed into the deep end with a ball and chain around her leg and the comment, "See, I told you the dumb bitch would never learn to swim." (June)

Georgina resigned as an affirmative action manager:

It was a dead-end job. There was never any support from the boys up top. It was always "do more with less" when I hardly had any resources to start with. It reached the point where I just had a gutful and got totally burnt out. Besides, I didn't want to be ghettoized as someone who could only do women's issues.

ORGANIZATIONS THAT MAKE AFFIRMATIVE ACTION WORK

Powell (1993) suggests that organizations respond to affirmative action in three main ways: proaction, reaction, and benign neglect. Proactive organizations practice affirmative action even in the absence of legislation. Reactive organizations merely respond to affirmative action in order to avoid litigation or because there are funding incentives. Organizations characterized by benign neglect institute affirmative action only if they are legally compelled to. Most of the organizations in this study fell into the reactive and/or benign neglect categories. However, a few organizations were proactive and were characterized by trust and cooperation between men and women. The senior mangers in these organizations had detailed knowledge of all men's and women's formal and informal abilities and publicly asserted a commitment to affirmative action. Annabelle's comments illustrate the outcome of sound leadership and management in these settings:

> The boss' strengths come from being efficient; he never wastes your time, although he always makes time to see you. But he's also a great "ideas" man. For example, his attitudes to women are unbelievably progressive! He's been absolutely proactive when it comes to women's issues. In fact, he's managed to mainstream them by prioritizing them, not just in our strategic plan but by actually giving women a go. He sits down with everybody and identifies strengths and weak points and the things we need to do to get on. Some of the guys jacked up at first, but he sat all of us down at a meeting and said he was not prepared to countenance discrimination or a waste of talent around here. It's the old thing about justice being done and being seen to be done. I just cringe when I see the conditions that women in other places work under. I think the worst scenario would be to be stuck in a women's sports promotion unit, unless your boss backs

you to the hilt, and we know that doesn't happen any-
where in this country! It's really unfair in those units . . .
the women there have to work so hard. Some of the men
they work with are threatened or try to undermine them,
while the public thinks they are a bunch of lesbian ratbags. It's a "lose-lose" situation. I am *so* lucky to be where
I am.

A man and a woman who were interviewed together provided a vivid illustration of how managerial (in)action on affirmative action affected organizational esprit de corps:

[Elspeth] The last boss was just terrific. From day one
he made it clear that the value of women was a high priority. [Rod] Yes, I think he gave some of the guys a bit of a
dong on the head at first, but he had all of the arguments
down pat on why we would be shooting ourselves in the
foot if we didn't start to bring more women in. [Elspeth]
The new guy is just the opposite. He's got no communication skills and is totally unapproachable, especially by
women. The only thing he ever says is, "The bottom line is
so and so." [Rod] Justice issues have gone by the board,
and the morale is lousy. [Elspeth] That's why I'm out of
here as soon as I find a better alternative. [Rod] Me, too.

SUMMARY

Few organizations had written affirmative action policies, and
most male managers believed that everyone was treated
equally. Insofar as affirmative action was pursued, it was
always in terms of getting individual women to the same starting line as men, rather than responding strategically to gendered, structural inequalities at work and home. Only a few
men articulated a strong commitment to affirmative action.
Most men had views on affirmative action that were hostile,
cynical, skeptical, and ambivalent. Even "soft" versions of affir-

mative action were often perceived as an attack on the principle of merit or were seen as anti-male, tokenism, or a radical-feminist scheme. Most men who were not opposed to or cynical about affirmative action tended to perceive it as "a women's issue," seeing the recipe for implementing it as simply to "add women and stir." Men perceived affirmative action as something that they did *to* or *for* women, rather than as a process that involved modifications for both sexes. None of the few organizations that did have affirmative action plans had placed issues of men and masculinity on the agenda. When affirmative action did receive support, it was seldom because of a commitment to gender equity or social justice. Even most advocates of affirmative action justified it on the basis of economic efficiency, sound human resource management, good public relations, or it ensured that the organization complied with the law and thus avoided litigation. Affirmative action managers exhibited a range of attitudes toward their work, most of them trying to balance idealism, pragmatism, and disenchantment.

Six

The Write Stuff?
Media Representations of
Affirmative Action in Australian Sport

THE MASS MEDIA are crucial in constructing hegemonic masculinity and emphasized femininity. While most journalists who cover sport are men, some women journalists have filed lawsuits in order to obtain the same access to the locker room enjoyed by their male counterparts. In an American study, 60 percent of women sports journalists reported facing sexual harassment from male colleagues (Eberhard and Myers 1988). In a case study of twenty-five Australian women sports journalists, fifteen indicated that gaining equal access to locker rooms was a major issue for them, and twenty-two had been refused entry to men's locker rooms at least once (Baird 1994).

Mass media representations of sport exemplify the twin processes of *symbolic annihilation* and *symbolic glorification* (Sabo and Jansen 1992). The former phrase alludes to the absence and underrepresentation of specific groups or portrayals that marginalize, trivialize, or stereotype their activities. The latter term refers to the presence and overrepresentation of certain groups or depictions that exalt their activities and experiences, even when these are anti-social and detrimental to themselves and to other groups. Given the heterosexist structures of labor, power, and cathexis in sport, it is not surprising that the mass media tend to symbolically annihilate sportswomen and gay men and symbolically glorify heterosexual sportsmen. In most countries, less than 5 percent of media coverage is devoted to women's sport and most newspaper items are placed in a separate section. Moreover, the coverage that does exist generally patronizes, stereotypes, or objectifies women. Editors and journalists often devote inordinate time and space to how beautiful and glamorous sportswomen are rather than to their physical and mental skills. This implies to audiences that sportswomen's achievements are frivolous and that women can be attractive *despite* being athletes.

Since men appear much more often than women in sport, it is one of the few contexts where gazing at men's bodies is both permitted and pervasive. But there is a profound taboo against making men voyeuristic objects, because in a heterosexist culture-gazing at objects is a male privilege, and thus a vehicle for objectifying, exploiting, and degrading women. The potential image of man-as-erotic object is superseded by that of man-as-machine, or warrior, which sustains auras of scientific technique and male perfection (Morse 1983). These characterizations are frequently complemented by militaristic descriptions of male athletes as "gladiators," "warriors," "field generals," "hit men," or "combatants" (McKay and Middlemiss 1995; Trujillo 1995). In summary, a prominent code of sports journalism is that male athletes should be admired for what they *do*, whereas female athletes should be desired for how they *look*. As Rowe (1990, 11) puts it:

> [The dominant] view is that champion athletes are male, except where they can be proved by their attractiveness and emotionality to be female, in which case they are females who also happen to play sport very well, although not as well as males. If this logic seems convoluted, then it is so because it is produced by the predominantly masculine culture of sport, of which its journalists are a manifest product.

Media "coverage" of sportswomen also contains structured *silences*, as it is rare to see reports, especially by men, about gender inequalities. However, there are two occasions when male journalists do pay a disproportionate amount of attention to sportswomen—in beating up a lesbian "angle" (Burroughs et al. 1995) and in attacking affirmative action for sportswomen. In this chapter I provide some examples of "groupthink" and symbolic annihilation with respect to male sports journalists' denigration of both women and affirmative action in Australian sport.

SPORTS JOURNALISM AND "GROUPTHINK"

In 1995 Jacqueline Magnay wrote a feature article on gender inequalities in Australian sport for *The Sydney Morning Herald*. Magnay was intimately acquainted with men's resistance to women's attempts to enter sport. In 1993 she lodged a formal complaint with the state Human Rights Commission after she was refused entry to the locker room of a football team. In her article, Magnay (1995) referred to the lack of respect that women receive from the public, media, and corporate sponsors, despite winning numerous individual and team championships at the international level. She also noted that one of the few instances where sportswomen do get attention is when they pose in skimpy attire for calendars or magazines. Three days later, one of her fellow journalists, Jeff Wells, responded by asking to be spared from "any more twaddle about women's sport," and "the crunch of the jillboot movement." He claimed that women athletes were "second-rate," and viewed pressure for gender equity in sport as "blackmail," "ludicrous," undemocratic, and contrary to the logic of the free market (Wells 1995).

Wells's vitriolic column was part of a litany of attacks that he and other male sports journalists have made on affirmative action initiatives in Australian sport. For instance, in 1990 three journalists from *The Courier-Mail* in Brisbane criticized the Queensland state government's creation of a Women's Sport Advancement Unit. In his article "Women athletes just don't pack 'em in like men," Lawrie Kavanagh (1990) alleged that the unit was comprised of "feminist ratbags . . . a bunch of misguided nitpickers with a giant chip on the shoulder," and painted an Orwellian scenario in which watching second-rate women athletes compete would become compulsory. Given the "obvious worldwide differences in temperament between men and women," the unit was dismissed as a waste of taxpayers' time and money on frivolous attempts to discourage sexist language and promote women's sport. He also claimed that women lacked "the physical strength and aggression to fill the stands," and ridiculed the suggestion that women were referred to in sexist terms by calling one swimmer the "princess of the pool" and another a "supermum." One of his colleagues, Paul Malone (1990), recounted a terrible dream in which his new sports editor, "Sally Suffragette," gave preference to women's sports over men's. Another journalist, Gary Smart (1990), told women that instead of complaining, they should use their looks to attract sponsorship.

However, it seems that women athletes cannot win even when they do "dress for success." At the 1990 Commonwealth Games an Australian woman athlete was verbally harassed by several male teammates. In an article in *The Canberra Times* ("Flaunt it, athletes, but cop the result"), Bill Mandle (1990) castigated sportswomen for adopting a "sleaze and glitz mode . . . derived from reference to one of the oldest of professions, designed to appeal to the most primitive of male instincts." He declared that such provocative behavior meant it was hypocritical for team managers to censure the men who harassed the woman. Like rape, there was "a case to be made for shared responsibility," but due to the "feminist error of monocausality," joint accountability had been removed from the agenda and "male lust alone" was unfairly deemed culpable.

In 1990 Wells trivialized an academic study of sexual discrimination in sport by Dennis Phillips (Wells 1989a,

1989b) and ridiculed a similar report by Sandy Gordon by caricaturing his clothing and then launching into a parody of gays and lesbians (Wells 1989c). He also remonstrated against a "feminist hatchet job" in *The Bulletin* [the equivalent of *Time* or *Newsweek*] written by a woman journalist ("with selective quotes from handy [male] academics") who suggested sport's macho code could be having some undesirable effects on children:

> How often can we endure the sort of dour feminist prong between the sagging buttocks of male esteem offered by *The Bulletin* this week? If women writers can drag "macho" out of the handbag anytime to degrade men for acting the way they have acted since time immemorial, but which has so recently been ruled inadmissible, we males need a female word (other than "bitchiness") which can be used to the same effect . . . Somebody, quickly, invent a feminine equivalent of "wank." (Wells 1990a, 34)

Shortly afterwards he dismissed Adrianne Blue's book on women's sport, *Grace Under Pressure*, as "mucho feminism." Wells preferred the violence, injury, high jinks, and drinking recorded in a book written by former rugby star Simon Poidevin. He speculated that the "grim amazons of revisionism" and "their male academic stooges" who had denigrated "macho bonding" would disapprove of Poidevin's masculine memoirs: "[Poidevin] could be cornered and gelded by an Adrianne Blue Machismo Elimination Unit, headed by gibbering . . . academics, at any moment" (Wells 1990b, 35).

In summary, these columnists consider sportswomen to be "ratbags," "supermums," "princesses," "whiners," "whores," "bitches," "wankers," "lesbians," "amazons" and "castrators," while research by academic men which demonstrates sexual inequalities in sport is merely propaganda by feminist flunkies. If equivalent language had been used to describe ethnic or racial minorities, these journalists conceivably could have been required to appear before the various antidiscrimination and human rights boards in Australia.

Male sports journalists also exhibited a "phallic panic" over the "Equity for Women in Sport Seminar," discussed in chapter 3. About 100 of approximately 300 representatives from across Australia who attended the event accepted an open invitation to participate in an episode of *Couchman* [similar to *Donahue*], which was advertised as focusing on why the media provided such scant coverage of women's sport. Speakers had addressed this very topic at the seminar, and examples of sexual prejudice and discrimination were documented in scores of more than 300 submissions to the committee. Thus, the producers and host could have screened an educational program by airing women's grievances. Instead, they reinforced ideologies of male superiority and engaged in a derisive display of "groupthink."

The front seats, quite literally, were given to a trio of men who did not attend the seminar but were flown in for the program: Ron Casey, former TV sports producer and populist radio commentator, whose political views are comparable to Rush Limbaugh's; Roy Masters, former football coach and sports journalist; and David Hookes, former member of the Australian men's cricket team and host of a radio sports show. From the outset, men's sport was defined as *the* exemplar which women ought to emulate, with the three "expert" guests arguing that women's sports deserved less coverage because they were intrinsically less interesting than men's sports. Not until five minutes into the program was the first woman in the audience even permitted to speak. The host, Peter Couchman, confined "debate" during the rest of the program to the premise that if women wanted to attract media attention they had to: market their sports according to commercial reality; promote sports that were as spectacular, exciting, and aggressive as men's; and exhibit more "sex appeal." The three men were allocated the majority of time, especially Casey, who repeatedly interrupted other speakers' remarks.

Both the seminar and the television program elicited misogynist reactions from several male journalists. In a subsequent column in *The Sydney Morning Herald* ("If you've got it, flaunt it, be ye a he or a she"), Masters described the women on *Couchman* who disagreed with him as a "hissing . . . colony of vipers masquerading as mathematics teachers." In fact, a replay clearly shows that it was not women jeering, but men and women laughing at Masters' convoluted statistical reasoning that 5 percent coverage of women's sport did not mean that men's coverage was 95 percent because 40 percent was devoted to the allegedly non-sexist sport of horseracing. He mocked non-sexist language: "Peter Couchman . . . should henceforth be called 'Couchperson,'" and reiterated that women athletes would get more coverage if they just raised hemlines, lost weight, changed hairstyles, and showed more flesh. He suggested women could emulate two male football players who had used sex appeal to sell their sports. Here we have the familiar strategy of permitting women to be "successful" only in terms defined by heterosexual men. In this case, how women athletes look as the objects of men's pleasure is deemed more important than what they do on sports fields.

Masters also claimed that since coverage of sport was market-driven, women had to sell themselves more strategically. This is hardly good news for women, given that the business world is neither female-friendly nor gender-neutral. Like nearly all institutions, it is overwhelmingly owned or controlled by men. Moreover, after pornography, the advertising industry probably portrays the most offensive images of women.

Other journalists, none of whom attended the seminar, also were reactionary. One of Masters' fellow columnists lampooned the "astonishing attempt in social engineering which will change the face of sport," and derided the use of counter-sexist language: "Welcome—brave, free, new, non-sexist new world" (Macdonald 1991, 76). Martin Warneminde of *The Bulletin* maintained there had been a "lack of reality" at the seminar: the critics had "put the cart before the horse," because "a sport gets the attention warranted by public interest" (Warneminde 1991a). In a subsequent column, he sarcastically asked if equal opportunity in sport was good news for nude male wrestlers (Warneminde 1991b).

In Brisbane, Gary Smart (1991) described the assertion that coverage of women's sport had not improved in the last decade as "a load of rubbish," despite reliable research to the contrary. Ironically, his column was adjacent to a photo of a finalist in the Indy Trophy Queen competition who posed in a jumpsuit revealingly unzipped from neck to mid-breast. Later, his colleague Wayne Smith (1991) attacked the "rampant feminism" of the federal minister for sport for wasting taxpayers' money on studying girls' self-esteem in sport:

> Last week [man] found himself hunted into the last corner of his last domain—sport. Once he was master of all he surveyed—the golf course, the football field, the gymnasium. Yet, one by one these strongholds fell, as Man was forced to cede joint tenancy to Woman.

A panic-stricken Wells (1991a) believed that the seminar posed a threat to the very fabric of Australian society. "Ratbag militants" and the "propaganda and big stick threats of airhead affirmative action plans" of the government were defying biology and desecrating the heritage of motherhood:

> It is a matter of instinct and choice, not equity and rights. The answer is in those wonderful female hormones that the feminist dupes prefer to ignore. They do make women different. Many of them actually want to have babies and put more time into raising families than other things, including sport. And in Australia, I believe they are the best mothers battling to raise the best families anywhere . . . social values hit the skids with the dismantling of the nuclear family in the name of "rights."

He also invoked a line made famous by—who else?—Clint Eastwood: "Go ahead promoters—make my day." Another quip for which Eastwood is renowned is apposite here: "A man's gotta know his limitations." One of Wells's major limitations is that his views on women belong to the 1890s instead of the 1990s.

THE "PARANOIA OF THE POWERFUL"

I see footballers as modern gladiators. Men of skill and bravery. Far from adding to the reservoir of blind hatred in society, their macho theatrics siphon off its poison. How many more rapes, muggings, and murders might there be without football to focus all that undirected frustration?

—Award-winning Australian journalist
David Bentley criticizing suggestions that
rugby league games were excessively violent.

Readers can make their own judgments about the professional standards of journalists who ignore the wealth of research on how the very medium from which they earn a living—language—is implicated in stereotyping, deprecating, and oppressing women (McKay 1992b, 1993). Psychoanalysts can diagnose what seems to this observer to be anti-intellectualism, male "hysteria," homophobia, misogyny, and castration complexes. More frightening is what this "paranoia of the powerful" reveals about the importance of sport in both reflecting and constituting hegemonic masculinity. That these men—and complicit editors, producers, and employers—can brazenly use sport to display such moral insensibility to defend men's privileges is surely sufficient in itself to warrant paying greater attention to the role of sport in constructing "groupthink" and sustaining the oppression of women—even in nonsporting settings.

One keynote speaker at the Equity for Women in Sport Seminar noted that while some might deem it indulgent to hold an event related to the problems of sportswomen, sport plays a crucial role in valorizing men's experiences and devaluing those of women. Moreover, these experiences can be, and all too often are, transferred to other areas of social life. Her observations are clearly demonstrated by the "groupthink" pervading male sports journalists' reactions to affirmative action initiatives—an anachronistic reaction, given that the recent steps toward equity now slowly being taken in sport began over a decade ago in other areas of Australian society. These misogynist assaults are a stark reinforcer of a warning made at the seminar by another keynote speaker, who said: "Those who have power never give it up without a long and intense struggle."

SUMMARY

It is no coincidence that these attacks by male journalists have occurred at a time when other retrograde antifeminist discourses abound in the popular media—the "feminism has gone too far" backlash. For instance, in 1995 the highest-circulating weekend supplement in the nation, *The Australian Magazine*, ran a cover story on the identity crisis allegedly facing Australian boys, and since 1992, its chief competitor, *Good Weekend*, has produced a special issue or cover story each year on various crises being experienced by Australian men. Most major daily newspapers and popular magazines have recently carried feature articles on issues like the demise of mateship, father-hunger, and men's putative obsolescence. Men have frequently been depicted in the media as "oppressed," "under siege," "embattled," "under fire," and "dodging bullets in the sex war"; "wildmen" are depicted on weekend retreats trying to retrieve their manhood that has been "stolen" from them by women; and affirmative action legislation is often blamed for boys' purportedly inferior educational performance and males' high morbidity and mortality rates.

This antifeminist discourse also needs to be located in the wider conservative cultural, political, and economic context of Australian society. For it comes at a time when: economic rationalism is ascendant in both the public and private spheres; there has been a protracted economic recession and high rates of unemployment; physical strength has ceased to be a requirement for most jobs; women are becoming more independent from men and making a few inroads into masculinist power structures; feminist and gay rights activists are constantly challenging hegemonic masculinity; and the importance of "traditional family values" is a pervasive motif among all the major political parties.

Similar hegemonic struggles are evident in Australia and North America as part of the "angry white men" discourse enunciated stridently by the men's rights movement and tacitly by the mythopoetic men's movement (Connell 1992; McKay and Ogilvie [in press]; Messner 1997; Pfiel 1995). According to Gibson (1994), Jeffords (1989, 1994), and McBride (1995), the emphasis on male bonding in the American popular media constitutes an ideological bulwark to the perceived threat of feminization and recuperates dissent by attempting to reinscribe men and women in their "natural" positions in the heterosexist gender order. In summary, for men and women attempting to eliminate "groupthink" in sport—and elsewhere—the power struggle appears set to go for at least a few more rounds.

Seven

Hegemonic Masculinity and the Gender Politics of Affirmative Action Policy Research

INTELLECTUAL WORK AND CULTURAL POLICY

A SOMETIMES ACRIMONIOUS controversy has recently emerged over the appropriate role of intellectuals working in the areas of cultural studies and cultural policy (cf. Bennett 1989, 1992; Cunningham 1992; Wark 1992). To date, much of the debate has focused on abstract issues like the advantages and disadvantages of "putting policy into cultural studies"—to use Bennett's (1992, 32) phrase—or if academics should be facilitators or critics of cultural policy. However, there has been a dearth of concrete accounts of tensions between the academics who conduct policy research and the organizations which fund and implement it. In this chapter I examine the response of ASC executives to two academic studies it funded on affirmative action policy. I also continue a theme from the previous chapter—the crucial function of the media in articulating masculine definitions of affirmative action in sport.

BACKGROUND TO THE REPORT

In 1990 the ASC designated affirmative action as a priority research area and funded three academic studies through its

Applied Sports Research Program (ASRP). All grant proposals are appraised by an expert research committee, which is composed of ASRP administrators and independent academics. I was funded to identify why there were so few women administrators in sporting organizations, with specific emphasis on the barriers to women's access and advancement. My findings were basically an Australian version of the data I presented in chapters 4 and 5. The findings were consistent with the many sport-related studies cited in chapter 3, a subsequent New Zealand inquiry by Cameron (1994) which replicated my work, and ensuing studies of the public and private sectors in Australia (Bellamy and Ramsay 1994; Canberra Bulletin of Public Administration 1994; Grant and Porter 1994; Karpin 1995; Wieneke and Durham 1992).

Given the government's official concern with Australian women's underrepresentation in administrative positions, I was keen to let their voices be heard and offer practical recommendations to the ASC. One of the serendipitous outcomes of the study was the number of unsolicited negative perceptions offered about the ASC's handling of affirmative action policy. As mentioned in chapter 3, criticisms of the commission had been aired publicly in 1991 at the Equity for Women in Sport Seminar. One keynote speaker (Timpson 1991) noted that the commission's own policies were wanting—a point that was not lost on many interviewees. Some respondents believed that the commission was hastily and cynically instituting its affirmative action plan mainly because of the pressure brought to bear on it by the inquiry. A glaring Achilles heel in the minds of many observers was that although the commission was supposed to be promoting affirmative action, none of its six top-level managers and only three of its twelve board members were women. Some interviewees also were aware that senior women in the commission had formed an informal support group to address what they believed was the commission's recalcitrance in implementing its own equity and justice policies. Moreover, the AIS had allowed its facilities to be used for a photographic session involving a female model which appeared in a recent issue of *Inside Sport,* a glossy monthly that resembles *Sports Illustrated's* swimsuit issue.

Although it behooved me to make the commission aware of the negative way in which it was perceived, I could see no point in publicly pillorying it, so I published only a few of the numerous disparaging comments that had been made. I assumed that the executive body would be concerned about the very existence of such perceptions and interested in how to respond to them openly and effectively. Therefore, I decided to alert the commission to the criticisms while making realistic recommendations that would enable it to respond convincingly. For instance, one of my main recommendations was that the commission should have important educational, funding, and steering functions to ensure that affirmative action principles were comprehensively integrated into its own organization and all ASC-funded organizations. The recommendations were compatible with those contained in recent national agendas for women, the Public Service Commission's Strategic Plan for Equal Employment Opportunity for the 1990s, and the Report of the Inquiry Into Equal Status and Equal Opportunity for Women in Australia. I also discussed the appropriateness of my recommendations during an extended interview with Michael Lavarch, who chaired the Inquiry into Equal Status and Equal Opportunity for Australian Women and later became Australia's Attorney General.

According to commission guidelines, ASRP reports are supposed to be written for a lay audience, so I did not use any abstract theory or present the statistical information I collected. Instead, I presented the data thematically and qualitatively. I included illustrations which I asked a professional artist to draw from cartoons that had appeared in academic, popular, and government publications on gender, management, and sport. I also inserted tables describing the general status of women in management and society, a poem used by Powell (1988) to describe the sexual politics of management, and Table 4.2.

The Commission's Response to the Report

> The history of men's opposition to women's emancipation
> is more interesting perhaps than the story of that eman-
> cipation itself.
>
> —Virginia Woolf

In August 1992 I submitted my report (Why So Few? Women Executives in Australian Sport) to the commission's national coordinator of sports research, who relayed it to two independent academics for assessment. After both assessors fully endorsed it, the coordinator issued invitations for a media launch of the report in Sydney by Ros Kelly, the minister of sport at Sports House. A few days before the scheduled launch, the national coordinator informed me that the commission's executive director, Jim Ferguson, had cancelled the launch because the report was "factually incorrect."

After sending a letter of inquiry to Ferguson, I received a joint telephone call from him and Bob Hobson, director of corporate services. I was informed that they actually did not consider the report to be factually incorrect, but were concerned about how it might be interpreted. Their "concern" was based on the following aspects of the report: it was not objective or valid because it only dealt with people's perceptions of barriers; it contained unfounded criticisms of the commission; and the above two issues could have embarrassed Kelly, who recently had experienced a public relations disaster over the release of an environmental kit. After some discussion, I agreed that Ferguson would send me a summary of his and Hobson's comments and I would consider whether it would be possible to incorporate them into a modified version of the report. Although I was suspicious of the cancellation of the launch, I agreed to study their remarks because the alterations they had been requested were minor.

A few days later, I discovered that the commission had upped the ante considerably. I received a five-page fax that reiterated and extended the items raised in our conversation and included additional criticisms that the report: (1) seemed to have "a heavy weighting towards the views of women rather than those of the men," and, therefore, could be criticized as a "put up job"; (2) was based on "selective quotations to support a preconceived view"; (3) seemed to suggest that men had been "written off"; (4) contained illustrations that were "offensive and possibly even libelous"; (5) was "heavily biased towards U.S. research"; and (6) suggested recommendations that were either inconsistent, impractical, or outdated. Regarding the last item, I was told that given the cost of child care, the commission was unsure how to implement my recommendation that it should play a pivotal role in coordinating efforts to make affordable, flexible, and quality child care available to employees, volunteers, and members of sporting organizations. Furthermore, I was informed that there had been a change in some figures I used in an appendix derived from one of the commission's own publications. The number of women board members in the commission had increased from three to four, and there now were thirty-five males (instead of forty) and eight females (instead of six) as either executives, section managers, or program coordinators. I also was advised that if "we were to restrict the numbers to executive/administrative positions, the ratio would be twenty male to eleven female."

It was stated that I accepted "uncritically all the things said" [by respondents] when there was "no argument to support [my] thesis." Ferguson elaborated that "some assessment would normally be required of the raw information," then asked: "Are the [respondents'] perceptions correct?" Paradoxically, he used the phrases "appears to be," "seems to me," "suggests to me," "I believe," "I think" and "we have perceived" over a dozen times in doubting the validity of data based on respondents" perceptions of their organizations, while simultaneously claiming to speak on behalf of the commission.

My first reaction was to tell the commission impolitely what it could do with the report. After all, I had excellent data that could be used for academic purposes. Moreover, given what I had uncovered in the study, I knew that the commission probably had damaged its credibility even further by canceling the launch. However, I decided to reply for three interrelated reasons. First, given the initial response, there seemed to be a very real possibility that the report would be suppressed when I believed it should have been officially accepted and acted upon. Second, I had interviewed past and present board members and managers of the ASC and knew that some of them had opinions that diverged greatly from those of Ferguson and Hobson. Third, if I had refused to make any alterations and the report had not been released, I would have been complicit in one of the most strident criticisms that many women managers relayed to me—the inability and unwillingness of men to listen to women's perceptions of the gender order in their organizations.

In October I wrote a detailed, point-by-point response, indicating that I actually had shielded the commission from extensive criticism and had made recommendations designed to enable it to counter this disapproval effectively. I also offered to take some of the commission's advice, even though I believed the changes it desired were not in its best interests. For instance, since the commission perceived that child care was both expensive and difficult to coordinate, I offered to make only a single recommendation that was weighted even more decisively in the commission's favor: "The ASC should be allocated the funds necessary to assist sporting organizations' plan for gender equity in sport."

Shortly afterwards I received a call from the head of commission's Women and Sport Unit, asking me to provide some "hard, quantitative data" and to reinstate the original recommendations, as the commission "would look foolish if it backed away from them now." I told her I would be happy to include statistical information and naturally agreed to reinstitute the original recommendations.

Just before completing the alterations, I received a telephone call from Roy Masters, the journalist mentioned in chapter 6, who appeared on *Couchman* and wrote disparagingly about the men and women who disagreed with him. He

asked for my comments on a story he was filing based on criticisms of the report that allegedly had been made by Ferguson
and Kelly. I told Masters that all of the accusations were
untrue. In his subsequent column, he stated that Ferguson:

> . . . cancelled the launch and returned the study to
> McKay, requesting that he resubmit the document,
> including the analysis on which his conclusions were
> based . . . Ferguson's complaint is that only about five
> pages of the report represent McKay's own thoughts.
> (Masters 1993, 76)

The minister was cited as being

> . . . pleased that a senior officer in her portfolio had read
> the report thoroughly before it was launched: "It is impor-
> tant to get the facts right, otherwise it can destroy your
> case . . . I don't want to discourage academic indepen-
> dence, but it is crucial that the methodology be correct if
> we are to implement recommendations based on univer-
> sity works." (Masters 1993, 76)

According to Masters:

> Most responses quoted in the study are made by women,
> the overwhelming impression . . . being that if a woman
> sport administrator made a comment, it was accepted as
> a truism by McKay . . . A detailed examination of the
> report demonstrates it is littered with perceptions and
> ignores analysis, making no attempt to quantify
> results . . . In my opinion, many of the recommendations
> are vague or out-dated . . . (Masters 1993, 76)

Masters noted that I endorsed the recommendation of
the Parliamentary inquiry regarding access to affordable, flexible, and quality child care "without making any input on the
costs or practicalities of this." He also wrote that I was "a

Canadian [who] also quotes liberally from American sources" and implied that I was guilty of "pigeon-holing females." [This referred to my use of table 4.2.]

If this incident was simply an example of a journalist beating up a story, it would not be worth mentioning. However, Masters is no ordinary journalist. He was a board member of the commission, a member of its Women and Sport Unit, and was involved in discussions of reports like mine at board meetings. He did not disclose any of these items or declare a conflict of interest in his newspaper column. I was reminded of numerous scenes from the British television comedy program, *Yes Minister*, by this attempt to discredit both me and the report. But my strongest reaction was an eerie feeling of déjà vu at being repudiated in a way that so many women interviewees had articulated.

Despite this incident, I was still determined to have the study endorsed, and I submitted a revised report that contained the following minor changes: (1) replaced "Executive Director, Sports Marketing Division and Sports Development Branch" with "Manager" on the desk name plates of the male figures in three of the illustrations; (2) changed the title of the poem from "How to Tell a Male Manager From a Female Manager" to "How to Tell a Male Manager From a Female Manager: A Humorous View"; (3) placed more emphasis on the importance of perceptions in organizations; (4) mentioned some sport-related studies from overseas (which had been included in my original grant proposal); (5) used more Australian examples in one of the tables; (6) provided details on the advantages of qualitative research; (7) fine-tuned aspects of some of the recommendations; (8) included the statistics in Appendix 3; (9) listed the commission's major affirmative action initiatives; and (10) recommended that the commission develop and promote its own human resource management program as an example of sound gender equity practice in sporting organizations.

The only mild concession I made was to replace the statement: "There was a widespread perception among both the men and women in this study that the ASC was at best contradictory and at worst hypocritical in its own [affirmative action] action" with: "Although the Commission has implemented a variety of [affirmative action] programs, many respondents were concerned about the absence of women in senior, decision-making positions who could serve as role models. The Commission currently is addressing this issue in its own [affirmative action] plan." I also enclosed a dozen anonymous interview excerpts, including some from current and former members of the commission, indicating the scathing nature of interviewees' comments about it and the minister. I stressed that I had made no changes to the data that appeared in the original document, as they constituted the backbone of the report, and I was not prepared to make any further alterations.

The commission accepted the revised report and invited me to attend a low-key media launch at the New South Wales Academy of Sport in Narrabeen on February 24, 1993. After returning from the launch I received a call from Charles Miranda of the *Canberra Times*, who inquired why the first launch was cancelled, why there had been two reports, and why had the launch been held at such short notice in Narrabeen instead of a more accessible venue. He then raised virtually the same allegations as Masters. I reiterated that the statements were incorrect and emphasized that if executives were making such statements, then they were contradicting the fact that the report had just been launched by an executive who publicly stated that it would be fully discussed at the next board meeting. Miranda's subsequent column (Miranda 1993) also resembled that of Masters' article. For instance, it focused on my Canadian background (at the time I had been an Australian citizen for most of the fifteen years that I lived in Australia), my use of some American references, asserted that the study was out-of-date, and claimed that "there is no evidence to support the author's conclusions." In our telephone conversation, Miranda alleged that male executives he had interviewed were "extremely unhappy with the emotional tone of the report." He claimed that my purportedly "emotive descriptions" were evident in the following statement in the document:

> If we think of the world of work as a pyramid, then most women are concentrated at the bottom in dirty, unsafe, tedious, insecure and low paying jobs. Regardless of their occupation, women usually are paid less than men even when they perform identical tasks.
>
> Although some men are taking greater responsibility for domestic labour, women perform most tasks during the 'second shift.' Studies have shown that husbands of working wives do almost as little in the way of domestic labour as husbands with spouses not in the workforce. (McKay 1992a, 4).

The commission's reaction to my report was not an isolated incident. Another academic submitted a grant proposal to investigate the experiences of women who facilitate and service sport played by others (Thompson 1991). As a condition of receiving funds, the ASRP insisted that men had to be included in her study when there was no precedent for ASRP projects to include both sexes. In fact, most ASRP studies have dealt almost exclusively with men. This focus is so taken for granted that reports are frequently published without noting that all participants are male. The rationale given to the investigator was that her study, based on qualitative data, would be strengthened by including men. Like my study, women's experiences presumably needed to be verified by men.

"TALKING TO THE ISAS" OR "DIALOGUE WITH THE DEAF"

In a controversial essay, Bennett (1989) has queried the received wisdom toward cultural studies and cultural policy by intellectuals. He argues that both the American and British versions of cultural studies have limited potential—the former is excessively aesthetic, while the latter subscribes to monolithic images of the state and/or capitalism and populist political strategies. In place of intellectual grandstanding, Bennett offers "a third course for cultural studies," producing knowledge that:

> . . . can be effectively used within actual existing spheres of cultural policy formation as constituted in the relations between governmentally constituted spheres of cultural management and the agencies and constituencies operative within those spheres. (7–8)

Elsewhere, Bennett (1992, 32) states that "putting policy into cultural studies" will entail:

> . . . talking to and working with what used to be called the ISAs [Ideological State Apparatuses], rather than writing them off from the outset and, then, in a self-fulfilling prophecy, criticizing them again when they seem not to affirm one's direst functionalist predictions.

Although I have reservations about some of the implications of Bennett's position, his remarks are extremely apposite to sport in Australia. Neglect of sport by critical policy analysts has meant that policy and research have been dictated by physical educators and sport scientists. Their awkward combination of liberal-humanism and instrumental rationality has legitimized state funding of programs like exercise management, corporate health, talent identification, elite sporting performance, and random drug testing (McKay 1991).

However, intellectuals wishing to "talk to the ISAs" should be aware that the latter tend to speak in a patriarchal vocabulary and listen with masculine and heterosexist ears. The tenacity of what Pateman (1988) calls the "fraternal social contract" is vividly illustrated by the above reactions of powerful men located in key areas of the media/state nexus. The commission's attempts to discredit my findings and the changes imposed on Thompson's research—especially when both studies were specifically targeted and funded by it to investigate gender inequalities—are sober reminders of men's formidable capacity to contain and resist women's experiences of gender oppression. The attempts to silence and rebuff women administrators' voices is also another clear example of the potent role sport plays both in reinforcing and constituting masculine hegemony in sport.

SUMMARY

Achieving equity for women in sport will not be an easy process, but will involve a need to change social attitudes as well as long-established practices. I am, however, determined to do all in my power to provide a special focus on the issue of women's involvement in sport and am confident that government and sporting organisations together can play a vital role in stimulating desired change.

—Ros Kelly, the then federal
minister for sport (ASC 1992, iii)

I can assure you that the Commission is fully committed to addressing the issues that face women in sport through research, programs, promotion, action to seek more female administrators, coaches, officials and through identifying and seeking to remove any impediments that we might find which are placed in the way of full participation by women.

—Jim Ferguson, Executive Director
of the ASC (HRSCLCA 1991, 1)

In 1992 Roy Masters was reappointed to the ASC board by Ros Kelly, and Bob Hobson was nominated as the ASC's senior officer responsible for equal employment opportunity. In 1993 Jim Ferguson was reappointed by Ros Kelly as the ASC's executive director and Kelly was reappointed minister for sport. Subsequently, Ros Kelly resigned from cabinet amid charges of ministerial incompetence and later retired from politics.

As indicated in the introductory chapter, profeminism is fraught with tensions. After hearing the presentation of a paper I gave on the above events at a national social policy conference, Lois Bryson, a former president of the Australian Sociological Association—who has published widely on feminism, sport, the state, and public policy—indicated that I might be contacted by one of her colleagues about presenting a brief version with a panel of women speakers which she was helping to organize for the women's section of the Australian Sociological Association's annual conference in 1993. Upon being contacted, I agreed to participate.

When asked to speak publicly about gender issues I am always cautious about being perceived as a colonizer of feminism. Thus, I always stress beforehand that I never speak on behalf of women and do not discuss women's issues unless a woman speaker is also invited. I felt that this protocol was unnecessary in this context because I knew I was likely to be in a huge gender minority at a gathering of feminists and had received an invitation from a highly-respected feminist sociologist. However, as I began my talk to an all-women audience of about 200, a small group stood up and left the room. The section organizers informed me afterwards that the group felt the event should have been for women only and had left to protest my presence. Although I was heartened by the number of women who subsequently urged me to continue my profeminist research, I was disturbed that I had offended others. I do not have any solution to this dilemma for profeminist men: to speak on behalf of women is unconscionable; to be silent about hegemonic masculinity is to be implicated in sustaining the status quo; to refrain from speaking about gender when invited by feminists for fear of offending other feminists undermines the opportunity to build alliances between feminists and profeminist men. Perhaps the best I can do is remind profeminist men that even when they "check with women" in conducting and presenting research (Spender 1981), there is no guarantee that their intentions will be unanimously welcomed.

Eight

One Cheer for
Affirmative Action

IT IS DIFFICULT TO CONCLUDE this study on an optimistic note, at least in the short term, given that affirmative action is under attack by neoliberal and neoconservative movements in most liberal-democratic states. In 1995 in the U.S., members of the disgruntled College Football Association and the National Wrestling Coaches Association formed an alliance that succeeded in having hearings held by a sympathetic Republican House subcommittee about the allegedly unfair basis of Title IX legislation. In the same year, Brown University appealed a federal court ruling that upheld an earlier decision that the institution had violated Title IX legislation by eliminating two women's teams in 1991. These attempts to roll back Title IX underscore the highly contested nature of affirmative action and some men's propensity to resist women's push for equality, despite abundant research showing that since the passage of Title IX, the number of women coaching intercollegiate and interscholastic sports in the U.S. has actually *declined* (Carpenter and Acosta 1991; Knoppers 1992; Lupiano 1994).

Despite its liberal inclination, affirmative action precipitates hostility and resentment because it challenges existing structures of inequality between men and women. It is, therefore, bound up with issues of change, specifically the politics of changing organizational cultures, changing men, and changing sport.

The Limits of Affirmative Action

This study suggests that affirmative action, as it is currently framed, will have limited success in facilitating more equitable gender relations in sport. Most sporting organizations lacked even basic affirmative action strategies and most that had them complied in a cynical, skeptical, or lip-service fashion. Even organizations that acted proactively toward affirmative action were underpinned by orthodox liberal definitions of fairness and a "politics of optimism," which assumes that equality can be achieved by getting more women to the same starting line as men (Blum and Smith 1998; Poiner and Wills 1991; Thornton 1994). But increasing the numbers of women in organizations will not necessarily change their masculine cultures and the stresses that women experience in combining work and family responsibilities. Therefore, if an organization attempts to recruit more women but retains affirmative action policies that are based on sameness rather than differences, then it is unlikely there will be much impact on what Cockburn (1991, 219) calls the "white male heterosexual and largely ablebodied ruling monoculture":

> The underlying theoretical assumption in the redistributive EEO or liberal reform model is that male-constructed and male-dominated organisational structures and processes are the yardstick against which success or failure to provide "equal employment opportunities" for women are measured. There is no questioning of the nature of the structures themselves and the contexts within which they are created, nor of the part they play in constructing and maintaining the very inequality we are attempting to eliminate. (Wieneke 1992, 137)

Affirmative action decontextualizes the masculine definitions of merit, skill, and performance that permeate most organizational cultures, and ignores the links between these intraorganizational features and the quantitative and qualitative differences between men's and women's family commitments. This liberal slant also allows individual men to file lawsuits claiming they have been victimized by affirmative action legislation and permits charges of "lowering standards," "tokenism," or "reverse discrimination" to be deployed whenever a "harder" version of affirmative action is mooted. This "harder" version also contains an undercurrent of victim-blaming by intimating that women are somehow deficient for not shattering the "glass ceiling" or taking advantage of affirmative action programs that are designed to help them "catch up" with men.

CHANGING ORGANIZATIONAL CULTURES

Several researchers have drawn on feminist principles and examples of successful feminist organizations in order to specify strategies for dismantling the institutional barriers that systematically favor men and disadvantage women in organizations (Burton 1991; Cockburn 1991; Iannello 1992; Martin 1993; Maier 1992). These analysts suggest that both men and women can benefit from using the following feminist practices to *transform* organizations:

- asking both the "woman question" and the "man question" in order to challenge androcentric practices that devalue and exclude women
- using feminist practical reasoning to deconstruct monolithic assumptions about organizational cultures and to decontextualize androcentric definitions of merit, skill, performance, and equal opportunity
- using consciousness-raising to affirm the collective nature of women's devaluation in organizations and to promote dialogical and cooperative schemes for transforming their subordinate status
- emphasizing cooperation, inclusion, and connectedness, while de-emphasizing cutthroat competition, individualism, and hierarchy

- fostering democracy and participation
- shifting structures of "power over" to practices of "empowerment," particularly among devalued and excluded groups
- encouraging an ethic of care within organizations
- individually and collectively mobilizing devalued groups, sensitizing men to the benefits of organizational change, and promoting corporate values that improve the community and physical environment.

In order to have a chance of succeeding, these kinds of strategies must occur in tandem with the following actions by both the state and trade unions: providing affordable, quality child care; reducing working hours; establishing equitable pro rata benefits for casual workers; strict, rather than cosmetic, enforcement of affirmative action legislation; and shifting from a rationality of the market to a rationality of care (Bacchi et al. 1992; Cockburn 1991; Else 1992; Hewitson 1994; Hyman 1992; Yeatman 1994).

Changing Men

It is unlikely that the kinds of changes mentioned above can be effected without simultaneously changing men. Martin (1993) contends that men can be persuaded to change if they can see the benefits of tapping into a larger pool of the human resources and the greater levels of productivity, efficiency, effectiveness, and loyalty that flow from supplanting the "male-normative" model of organizations with a feminist one. Yet, is important to emphasize just how resistant men are to women's entry into organizations (Cockburn 1991). According to Goode (1992), relations of inequality between men and women specifically reflect relations between superordinates and subordinates in general (e.g., social classes, ethnic groups, and castes). Consequently, men display attitudes and behavior that can be found among all superordinates:

- men tend to assume that their achievements are the just result of innate superiority rather than benefits that accrue from belonging to a superordinate group
- since women are more constrained by men than men are by women, women tend to observe men's behavior much more closely than men observe women's behavior
- men tend to reject any suggestion that they conspire to oppress women
- men tend to exaggerate even minor gains by women and to underestimate the institutionalized privileges that they continue to hold.

Thus, men resist when their hegemony is challenged by affirmative action as it threatens the status quo:

> . . . [men's] resistance is that of dominant groups throughout history; they enjoy an exploitive position that yields them an unearned profit in money, power, and prestige. Why should they give it up? (Goode 1992, 288)

Goode maintains that women's inexorable quest to become fully liberated will combine with a blend of moral, emotional, material, technological, and sexual forces to defeat men's resistance in the long run. In the short and medium terms, an important task is to politicize and transform hegemonic masculinity by making men's power "visible"—to name men *as men* in organizations (Collinson and Hearn 1994). There is a tremendous amount of work to be done simply to make many men realize that structured gender inequalities even exist in their everyday lives. Although nearly all women I interviewed strongly resented the masculine cultures in their organizations, they were appreciative of *individual* men who did act equitably. This included men who had mentored them, were proactive about affirmative action, and supported women's grievances. As we have seen, a handful of men were critical of the organizational status quo and supported affirmative action.

I do not wish to be excessively optimistic about these atypical cases. The defensive reactions to reports on affirmative action by the ASC and the misogynist and homophobic responses of Australian sports journalists to affirmative action initiatives highlight the difficulty of hoping that powerful men in sport will support affirmative action. But some men can advance equity, and they should be included in the "practical alliances" that are needed to create equitable organizational structures (Cockburn 1991).

One important short-term strategy in this respect is getting issues of men, masculinity, sexuality, sexual harassment, and leadership on affirmative action agendas, especially in management training programs (Bluckert 1989; Hearn 1989, 1992, 1994; Ruth 1989; Simmons 1989). A medium-range project is to link these internal organizational issues with profeminist, gay-affirmative, male-positive movements among men, as well as forging strategic alliances with women, people with disabilities, and people of color (Messner 1997; Weeks 1985). In short, privileged men need to empathize with the struggle of devalued and excluded groups to demonstrate that the politics of equality and the politics of difference are compatible, rather than opposing, principles (Bell et al. 1993; Gatens 1992; hooks 1984; Martin 1994; Young 1990).

CHANGING SPORT

Men—particularly sports administrators and coaches—have the capacity to eradicate sexism and sexual violence in sport. Administrators and coaches can require male athletes to complete violence prevention programs (Katz 1995) and encourage them to join profeminist groups like Men Against Sexual Assault, National Organization of Men Against Sexism, and the White Ribbon Campaign.

Messner and Sabo (1994) claim that there is nothing inherent in sport that makes male athletes harass and rape women. Rather, the way in which sports are organized to glorify violence and devalue and objectify women produces the "groupthink" that leads male athletes to harass and rape. One way men can start to change both themselves and sport is to practice the 11-point strategy suggested by Messner and Sabo in Table 8.1. Similarly, Lenskyj (1992b) has provided recommendations and checklists that administrators, coaches, and athletes can use to be proactive toward eliminating sexual harassment in sport (see Table 8.2).

TABLE 8.1
Changing Men through Changing Sports: An 11-point Strategy*

---

1. Be a Friend to Your Body: Resist definitions of masculinity that put bodies at risk, glorify pain, and promote or ignore injury. Develop athletic potential in ways that are challenging but not physically harmful. Renounce painful and risky training practices. Confront and report instances of verbal or physical abuse of players by coaches. Reject locker-room clichés that encourage athletes to disregard the limits and vulnerability of their bodies, such as "No pain, no gain," and "You gotta pay the price to win."

2. Stop Excessive Violence in Sport: Change the rules and challenge the underlying values of games that promote violence and excessive aggression. Developing less aggressive forms of sports will make them safer for athletes and erode harmful cultural equations between sports, masculinity, and violence.

3. Recognize Men's Issues in Sports: Identify men's issues in sports. Pro-feminist men have advocated an end to rape, domestic violence, sexual abuse, and sex discrimination in the workplace, and other forms of oppression of women by men. Yet we have been very slow to recognize that men also oppress other men. Why is it that pro-feminist men can immediately recognize the injustice of a man beating his wife, yet muster only a vague criticism of two men beating the pulp out of each other in a boxing ring?

4. Resist Locker-Room Sexism: Refuse to laugh at sexist jokes in the locker room. Challenge your friends when they ridicule women or treat them as sex objects. Don't let bullies get away with intimidating younger or weaker boys. Confront them face-to-face, or get help from coaches, administrators, or school officials.

(continued on next page)

TABLE 8.1 *(continued from last page)*

---

5. Fight Sexism in the Media: Do not tolerate sexism in the sporting media. Phone or write television or radio stations that promote sexist stereotypes—female athletes as sex objects, or male athletes as "dumb jocks." Insist that newspapers provide equal coverage for women's and men's sports. Boycott companies that use sexist images of male or female athletes to market their products.

6. Teach Young Athletes Non-Sexist Values and Practices: Parents, coaches, P.E. teachers, and community groups can teach children to recognize and question gender stereotypes in sports, such as in comments like these: "Sports are for boys," "Jane is good at baseball because she's a tomboy," "You throw like a girl," "This game wasn't made for sissies," or "He hits like a pussy." Work with young people to redefine sports values and practices. Provide children with opportunities to participate in a wide range of competitive and cooperative sporting experiences.

7. Work for Affirmative Action in Sport: Seek to develop affirmative action in youth sport programs, school sport, and community sport. Help make the fundamental principle of affirmative action a visible, dynamic, and ongoing dimension of program planning and evaluation.

8. Confront Homophobia and Heterosexism in Sports: Recognize that homophobia and heterosexism are forms of prejudice. Support educational efforts that aim to eliminate homophobia in sports, and support moves by gay and lesbian athletes to "come out," and new athletic institutions such as the Gay Games.

9. Become an Advocate for Minority-Group Athletes: Help people of color avoid exploitation in sports. Insist that schools and community organizations link the sporting activities and dreams of minority-group youth to solid educational agendas. Develop ways to use sport as a tool for raising the educational aspirations and achievements of minority-group youth.

10. Get More Women Involved in Sports: Work to maximize women's participation in coaching and administration. Great numbers of women in leadership positions will provide girls with more role models to look up to. Male athletes will also benefit from increased opportunities to observe and work with women in non-traditional roles. Stereotypes of masculinity and femininity, especially as they have been promulgated in sports, will break down with more female leaders. Mutual respect and cooperation between the sexes in sport will be encouraged. And including

---

(continued on next page)

TABLE 8.1 *(continued from last page)*

more women of color in sports leadership positions will promote understanding and respect for racial and ethnic group members.

11. Push the "Man Question": Men need to be more assertive about taking on the "man question" in feminist theory. In the past, men have sometimes felt like intruders in women's studies circles. There is an important difference, however, between interloping on the professional opportunities of female academics (who *already* face formidable sex discrimination) and tapping the feminist paradigm for inspiration and guidance.

Source: M. Messner and D. Sabo, *Sex, Violence and Power in Sports: Rethinking Masculinity* (The Crossing Press, 1994).

TABLE 8.2
Recommendations and Checklists
on Sexual Harassment
for Coaches and Athletes*

Recommendations

- All NSOs should develop, publicize, and implement zero tolerance sexual harassment policies
- Coaching certification programs should include information and awareness-raising sessions for all coaches on the issue of sexual and homophobic harassment
- Coaching certification programs should include thorough coverage of eating disorders, including guidelines for coaches
- Mandatory workshops on these issues should be provided for coaches who are already certified
- Professional journals should publish special issues on sexual harassment and eating disorders
- Women's committees within NSOs should develop support networks for girls and women who have experienced harassment

THE CHILLY CLIMATE CHECKLISTS

Every girl and woman has the right to be safe while she is participating in a sport or fitness activity. The concept of safety goes beyond physical surroundings, although these must also be considered. There are other aspects

(continued on next page)

TABLE 8.2 *(continued from last page)*

of the environment which are less tangible, but equally important for girls' and women's safety. These are factors which contribute to the "chilly climate" which girls and women experience in many sport contexts. The checklists below are designed to raise awareness about safety issues for girls and women in sport and physical education activities.

Coaches' Checklist

The General Climate

- Do you take any steps necessary to make the facilities safe for girls and women?
- Do you report poor lighting, graffiti, litter, or broken windows to the appropriate authority?
- Do you monitor male spectators' behavior?
- Do you put a stop to sexually harassing behavior by spectators?
- Do you remove any offensive pictures (nudes, "pin-ups") or graffiti from the walls?
- Are you prepared to deal with sexual harassment or sexual assault emergencies?
- Do you understand what constitutes a reportable offense?
- Do you act as an advocate on women's safety issues?

Your Personal Behavior

- Do you look at female athletes' bodies in ways that are intrusive or in any way inappropriate?
- Do you make derogatory or demeaning remarks about girls and women?
- Do you call adult women "girls"? Do you refer to the team as "my girls"?
- Do you make sexist, racial, or homophobic jokes?
- Do you make sexual innuendoes about women?
- Do you make humiliating comments about athletes' bodies or body weight?
- Do you touch female athletes in inappropriate ways?
- Do you understand the difference between physical contact that is appropriate in the sport context (e.g., spotting in gymnastics) and inappropriate physical contact?
- Have you ever asked a female athlete to go on a date?
- Have you ever given preferential treatment to a female athlete (e.g., selecting her for the team) in exchange for sex?

(continued on next page)

TABLE 8.2 *(continued from last page)*

Female Athletes' Checklist

The General Climate

- Do you feel safe training and practicing in this facility?
- Do you feel safe as you travel to and from this facility?
- Is the facility well maintained (e.g., good lighting, no broken windows, litter, or graffiti)?
- Are there offensive pictures (e.g., nudes, "pin-ups," cartoons) or graffiti on the walls?
- Is the security system adequate (e.g., security guards, emergency telephones)?
- Do male spectators act in harassing ways, either verbally or non-verbally, while you are training or practicing?
- Are instructors and other personnel equipped to deal with sexual harassment or sexual assault emergencies?

The Male Coach

- Does the coach look at you in ways that make you feel uncomfortable?
- Does he make derogatory or demeaning remarks about women?
- Does he make sexist, racist, or homophobic jokes or comments?
- Does he make humiliating comments about your body or body weight?
- Does he touch you in inappropriate ways?
- Does he understand the difference between physical contact that is appropriate in the context of sport (e.g., spotting in gymnastics) and inappropriate physical contact outside the sport context?
- Has the coach ever asked you to go out on a date with him?
- Has he ever suggested that he would treat you preferentially (e.g., select you for the team) if you had sex with him?
- How safe would you feel if you were alone with the coach?
- Did you check out this coach's record regarding his attitude towards women, before deciding to train with him?
- Did you talk to other women in the club/team about his treatment of female athletes?

Source: H. Lenskyj, "Sexual Harassment: Female Athletes' Experiences and Coaches' Responsibilities. *Science Periodical on Research and Technology in Sport* (12, 6: 1–5).

Who and What Is Changing Whom?

> The master's tools will never dismantle the master's
> house.
>
> —Lorde 1979, 110

Cohn (1987, 714) notes that it is pleasurable and seductive for women to "seemingly beat the boys at their own game." But overcoming women's oppression in sport and society is unlikely to be achieved by a minuscule number of white, affluent, heterosexual women trying to compete on men's terms and then being "creamed off" (Kenway 1995). As Stolcke (1981, 46) puts it, "To propose that women have first to become like men in order to become free is almost like suggesting that class exploitation might be ended by making it possible for workers to become capitalists." Or to borrow an apposite phrase from Allen (1990, 34), this strategy merely helps to reproduce a gender order which is based on "males judging their own value in terms of competitive performance against other males, and females judging their own value in terms of the degree to which they are valued by males."

As Carpenter and Acosta (1991, 23, 27) comment, there is also a prospect of women being co-opted:

> [Women] are playing in a game that uses men's rules on a playing field designed for men with male referees who have strong loyalty to the home team. The men have had decades more practice. Even if the women become more skilful than the men at the men's games, they might win only to find that winning has cost them their souls.

Furthermore, the corporate-feminist scenario does not democratize sport by encouraging diversity and criticism and has little relevance to most aboriginal, migrant, ethnic, aged, widowed, disabled, lesbian, and women with dependent children. Few corporations are interested in these "target groups." Rather than emulating the hegemonic male model, women (and men) could follow the example of feminist grass roots movements and organizations that emphasize cooperation, fun, and intrinsic outcomes, and try to combat heterosexism, homophobia, and sexual harassment in sport (Bennett 1993; Birrell and Ritcher 1987; Griffin 1991, 1992; Lenskyj 1991; Theberge 1987). In this way, instead of being a regime of self-management and self-surveillance, participation in sport could perhaps become a vehicle for individually and collectively engendering what MacKinnon (1987) has felicitously called women's *self-possession.*

The disproportionate number of women who manage affirmative action programs in sporting organizations in Australia, Canada, and New Zealand face a profound dilemma. On the one hand, they are criticized by their sisters who are committed to grass roots politics for pandering to masculine and corporate interests and paving their own career paths. There are, of course, few opportunities for women to command security, earn high salaries, and wield power at work. So, as Lynch (1984, 40) argues, it is "divisive nonsense," to reprimand "femocrats" for "selling out."

On the other hand, the masculine and managerial discourses of the state have co-opted many of these women's attempts to address gender inequalities (Dowse 1988, Eisenstein 1991, Franzway et al. 1989, Lynch 1984; Steinberg 1998; Watson 1991, 1992; Yeatman 1990). According to Hall, the evolution of CAAWS is an instructive example of the schizoid political predicament faced by women's sport organizations she has studied in Australia, Canada, the United Kingdom, and the United States—whether to promote *sport for women* or *women in sport*:

> The former denotes a more radical feminist perspective in the sense that CAAWS is a women's organization that promotes its aims through sport; the latter represents a distinctly liberal approach which seeks to improve the lot of women already in sport through a sports organization for women. (Hall 1994, 54)

155

Hall argues that a combination of the masculine domination of sport, the traditionally conservative political views of sportswomen, and pressure from the state have depoliticized CAAWS's activities and gradually moved it toward a liberal-feminist orientation. For instance, in 1990 the office of the Canadian Secretary of State withdrew its support, which prompted CAAWS to be relocated to the Sport, Fitness and Administration Centre in Ottawa. This shift made it even more difficult for CAAWS to be at arm's length from SC. Hall claims that despite some of CAAWS's pro-lesbian and anti-homophobic initiatives, attempts to keep these and other mainstream feminist issues on the agenda (e.g., sexual harassment, violence against women, the politics of difference) have encountered resistance both from within and outside the organization.

Moreover, there has been a tendency for women's sporting organizations to emulate the hierarchical aspects of bureaucratic organizations, as professional experts skilled in marketing, business administration, and management supplant the grass roots volunteers. In a Canadian study, Hall et al. (1989, 42) predicted that affirmative action issues would be co-opted by the rational-bureaucratic culture and masculine discourses which dominate sporting organizations:

> From a radical feminist perspective . . . the problem of change for the betterment of women (and men) is how to create change so that the values of people in power are not necessarily the values of a fundamentally homogeneous group of specifically white, middle-aged men of privilege. If women who are imitation men are placed in these positions, fundamental change will not occur.

It would be a retrograde step to dismiss affirmative action programs in sport by the state because they do not cater to the "needs of all women"—this is an impossible task. As Connell (1990a, 536) notes, affirmative action initiatives provide some leverage for some women even if they are not connected with "a more radical form of engagement with the state." For instance, many of the programs and publications of the ASC, HC, and SC have presented alternatives for women, albeit for a restricted audience. Nevertheless, the assimilation of affirmative action into the mutually reinforcing discourses of corporate masculinity, corporate femininity, corporate-managerialism, and liberalism means that the state is complicit in a process by which "malestream" sport is doing more to change women than women are to change sport.

Summary

This study suggests three main directions for further research. First, there is the possibility of using the perspectives of pro-feminism and social constructionism to carry out empirical investigations of other aspects of sport (e.g., coaching, media representations, violence, officiating, sport science, physical education). Despite the fact that sport is a key terrain of gender struggle and resistance, and an important site for disciplining and sexualizing bodies, it has received comparatively little attention from scholars working in the area of men's studies and women's studies. Although my investigation has provided some in-depth insights into articulations among gender, labor, power, cathexis, affirmative action, sporting organizations, and the state, it was restricted to people in managerial positions from mainly heterosexual, middle-class, able-bodied, Anglo backgrounds. Further studies of how gender regimes in sport interact with other social divisions—class, ethnicity, race, age, region, nation, sexualities—are needed (cf. Birrell 1990; Birrell and Cole 1990; Bredemeier 1992; Dunk 1991; Foley 1990; Hall 1996; Kane 1995; Klein 1993, 1995; Phillips 1987; Pronger 1991; Smith 1992; Trujillo 1991).

Second, there is the potential for researchers to analyze gender, labor, power, and cathexis in other contexts (Holloway 1994; Krenske 1993).

Finally, affirmative action needs to be studied in other contexts by interrogating men's privileges and exclusionary practices rather than women's "disadvantage" or "underepre-sentation" (Bacchi 1993; Cockburn 1991; Kenway 1995; Overall 1987; Shaver 1990; Witz 1990). As I have tried to demonstrate in this book, "studying up" the gender order can help to politicize and transform hegemonic masculinity by unmasking its gender-neutral status and making its power "visible"—not just in sport, but in all institutions.

Appendix 1:
Organizational Affiliations of Interviewees

*Commonwealth Agencies, Departments,
and Statutory Bodies*

Australian Sports Commission (including ASC Board and
Executive, Australian Coaching Council, Australian Institute of
Sport, Women and Sport Unit)
Australian Sports Drug Agency
Department of the Arts, Sport, the Environment, Tourism and the
Territories

State and Territory Departments

Australian Capital Territory
Office of Sport and Recreation

New South Wales
Department of Sport, Recreation and Racing
NSW Academy of Sport
Hunter Academy of Sport

Northern Territory
Office of Sport, Recreation and Ethnic Affairs

Queensland
Department of Sport, Tourism and Racing (including Women's Sports
Promotion Unit)
Queensland Academy of Sport

South Australia
Department of Recreation and Sport
South Australian Sports Institute

Tasmania
Department of Tourism, Sport and Recreation
Tasmanian Institute of Sport

Victoria
Department of Sport and Recreation
Victorian Institute of Sport

Western Australia
Ministry of Sport and Recreation
Western Australian Sports Council
Western Australian Institute of Sport
Western Australian Sports Federation

National Sports Organizations

All Australia Netball Association
Amateur Boxing Union of Australia
Australian Canoe Federation
Australian Confederation of Sports for the Disabled
Australian Cycling Federation
Australian Lacrosse Council
Australian Rugby Football Union
Australian Commonwealth Games Association
Australian Masters' Games
Australian Olympic Committee
Australian Society of Sports Administrators
Australian Sports Medicine Federation
Australian Touch Association
Australian Volleyball Federation
Australian Women's Cricket Association
Australian Women's Hockey Association
Australian Women's Soccer Association
Australian Yachting Federation
Basketball Australia
Confederation of Australian Sport
National Ice Skating Association of Australia
Orienteering Federation of Australia

Special Olympics - Australia
Universities Sports Association
Sportswomen's Association of Australia

Other Organizations

ACT Association for Women in Sport and Recreation
MLC Junior Sports Foundation
Rothmans Foundation
Western Australian Women in Sport Committee
Western Australian Women's Sport Foundation

CANADA

Sport Canada
Canadian Association for the Advancement of Women in Sport
and Physical Activity

NEW ZEALAND

Hillary Commission for Sport, Fitness and Leisure

Appendix 2:
Questionnaire on the Status of Women Sport Executives

I am completing a study of affirmative action policies in sport. As part of the study, this questionnaire is being sent to both men and women in your organization. The questionnaire is designed to obtain managers' views on how men and women advance in sporting organizations. The information you provide will be used solely for statistical analysis and will be kept strictly confidential.

Please complete the questionnaire and return it in a sealed envelope to the receptionist within 48 hours. I will be contact you within 24 hours to arrange a follow-up interview that takes about 1 hour.

Yours sincerely,

Dr. Jim McKay
Department of Anthropology and Sociology
The University of Queensland
Queensland
AUSTRALIA

INSTRUCTIONS

1. Please TICK (✓) or PRINT the appropriate response to each question.
2. An *executive* refers to someone holding a high-ranking position (eg, chairperson, coordinator, director, head coach, manager, president, secretary, treasurer).

3. A *sporting organization* refers to an association, board, club, corporation, council, federation, league, society or union (eg, Australian Rowing Council) or government board, commission, department, division, institute, section or unit (eg, Australian Sports Commission).

NAME _____

PART 1: YOUR BACKGROUND AND FUTURE PLANS

1. Please print the title of the position(s) you currently hold in your organization:

_____

2. Which of the following items best describes how you got the above position?

Tick ONE only:

__ By competition (winning or qualifying)
__ By appointment
__ By acting in the position
__ By secondment
__ By transfer
__ Change from temporary to permanent position
__ Other, please specify _____

3. How did you first find out about the above position?

Tick ONE only:

__ Advertisement in newspaper
__ Advertisement in public service gazette
__ Someone in the organization told me about it
__ Other, please specify _____

5. Tick which of the following items was the most important in getting you the above position:

Tick ONE only:

__ Educational qualifications
__ Opportunity to act in the position prior to appointment

__ Access to appropriate training for this position
__ Personal traits
__ Knowing someone in the organization
__ Previous work experience
__ Background as an athlete
__ Had a senior person/mentor looking out for my interests
__ Other, please specify _____

6. Aside from your current position, list all others you hold and have held in this or other sporting organizations since 1988. Please indicate the years you were involved, the specific organization, the level at which you held the position and the status of each position:

Year(s)	*Organization*	*Position & Level*	*Status*
eg: 1988-90	Australian Swimming Association	State Treasurer	Paid, part-time

1. _____
2. _____
3. _____

7. Please indicate any executive positions you hold in non-sporting organizations:

eg:	*Position & Level*	*Organization*
	National Secretary	Amnesty International

1. _____
2. _____
3. _____

8. Please indicate if you are competing or have competed in sport at the provincial, national or international level.

	Sport	*Highest level of competition*
eg:	Gymnastics	International

1. _____
2. _____
3. _____

9. Which of the following items represents your plans for the next 3 to 5 years?

Tick ONE only:

__ Maintain my current position (Go to 11)
__ Retirement (Go to Part 2)
__ Seek reassignment in my organization
__ Leave my organization temporarily
__ Resign to seek a position elsewhere
__ Seek promotion in my organization
__ Other, please specify _____

10. Why do you want this change?

Tick ALL that apply:

__ To get a higher salary
__ To gain more experience
__ To have more responsibility
__ To have a more challenging job
__ It is the next logical step in my career plan
__ To spend more time with my family
__ I have problems with child care
__ I cannot stand my job
__ I do not get along with my superiors
__ To get away from sexual discrimination or harassment
__ To get away from prejudice against gays and/or lesbians
__ To get away from ethnic/racial/religious prejudice
__ Other, please specify _____

11. Why are you not seeking a change?

Tick ALL that apply:

__ I need more experience
__ I do not have enough education to change my status
__ I have already reached the highest level for my skills
__ A new job will not allow sufficient time for family responsibilities
__ I do not want added work responsibilities
__ I do not want to change my child care arrangements
__ The competition process is too stressful
__ I do not think there will be any jobs

__ I lack confidence in my abilities
__ I have already reached my career goal
__ I am satisfied with my current position
__ Other, please specify _____

PART 2: DEMOGRAPHIC INFORMATION

1. Year of birth: 19 __ __

2. Sex: Male __   Female __

3. Marital status:

__ Single
__ Married
__ Living with a partner
__ Separated
__ Divorced
__ Widowed

4. Which of the following best describes your current home situation?

__ Head or joint head living with partner and with children or dependents
__ Head or joint head living with partner and without children or dependents
__ Single parent living with children or dependents
__ Single and sharing with another adult(s).
__ Single and living with parents.
__ Single and living alone
__ Other, please specify _____

5. Have you ever actively raised or are you presently raising a child/children?

__ No (Go to 6)
__ Yes, please indicate the ages of all children and tick whether they are current or former dependents:

	Age	Currently Dependent	Formerly Dependent
Child # 1	—	—	—
Child # 2	—	—	—
Child # 3	—	—	—
Child # 4	—	—	—
Child # 5	—	—	—
Child # 6	—	—	—
Child # 7	—	—	—
Child # 8	—	—	—

6. What is the highest level of education you have completed?

__ Less than high school
__ Completed high school
__ Completed certificate/diploma at a college or school
__ Completed Bachelor's Degree
__ Completed Master's Degree
__ Completed Doctorate Degree
__ Other, please specify _____

7. How would you describe your social class background?

__ Lower class
__ Working class
__ Middle class
__ Upper class

8. Do you consider yourself as having a religion?

__ No
__ Yes, my religion is: _____

9. Please indicate the country of birth of your:

Mother _____ Father _____ Self _____

If NOT born in this country, where were you born? _____

10. Apart from belonging to this country, please indicate if you consider yourself to belong to a particular ethnic, racial or religious group (eg, Chinese, Dutch, Greek, Maori, Irish, Italian, Jewish):

_____

PART 3: YOUR EXPERIENCES WITH SEXUAL DISCRIMINATION IN SPORT

1. Have you ever been aware of direct or indirect preferential treatment of MEN in recruitment, selection or promotion to positions in sporting organizations?

__ No (Go to 2)
__ Yes, please describe the circumstances but do NOT provide the names of any individuals concerned:

_____

_____

_____

2. Have you ever been aware of direct or indirect discrimination against MEN in recruitment, selection or promotion to positions in sporting organizations?

__ No (Go to 3)
__ Yes, please describe the circumstances but do NOT provide the names of any individuals concerned:

_____

_____

_____

3. Have you ever been aware of direct or indirect preferential treatment of WOMEN in recruitment, selection or promotion to positions in sporting organizations?

__ No (Go to 4)
__ Yes, please describe the circumstances but do NOT provide the names of any individuals concerned:

_____

_____

_____

4. Have you ever been aware of direct or indirect discrimination against WOMEN in recruitment, selection or promotion to positions in sporting organizations?

__ No (Go to 5)

__ Yes, please describe the circumstances but do NOT provide the names of any individuals concerned:

_____
_____
_____

5. Have YOU ever experienced direct or indirect preferential treatment in recruitment, selection or promotion to positions in sporting organizations?

__ No (Go to 6)
__ Yes, please describe the circumstances but do NOT provide the names of any individuals concerned:

_____
_____
_____

6. Have YOU ever experienced direct or indirect discrimination in recruitment, selection or promotion to positions in sporting organizations?

__ No (Go to 9)
__ Yes, please describe the circumstances but do NOT provide the names of any individuals concerned:

_____
_____
_____

7. If you have been discriminated against, what was your response?

Please tick ALL that apply:

__ I did nothing because it was not important enough to bother me
__ I did nothing because I was afraid of reprisals
__ I did nothing because I thought any response would be futile
__ I complained orally to my superiors
__ I submitted a written complaint to my superiors
__ Other, please specify _____

8. If you complained, please comment on how satisfactorily the grievance was resolved:

_____
_____
_____

9. People are sometimes denied career advancement (eg, promotion, secondment, transfer, training, travel) for reasons that have nothing to do with their skills, qualifications or experience. Have YOU ever been denied advancement in sporting organizations for any of the following reasons?

Tick ALL that apply:

__ I had a conflict with my superiors
__ I did not want to work overtime/set hours/shifts
__ I was too young
__ I was too old
__ I was pregnant or planning to become pregnant
__ I am a woman
__ I am a man
__ I am a bisexual, gay or lesbian person
__ I am a member of an ethnic, racial or religious group
__ I am a person with disabilities
__ I had young children or other dependents at home
__ I worked part-time
__ I was divorced/separated
__ I was a single parent
__ I objected to sexual discrimination or harassment
__ I had taken maternity/paternity or child care leave
__ I had taken education/training leave
__ I had taken long term disability/sick leave
__ I could not relocate or travel
__ There was "glass ceiling" in the organization
__ I did not know "the right people"/was not part of "the right group"
__ Other, please specify _____

PART 4: HOW YOU PERCEIVE YOUR ORGANIZATION

1. Below are some common statements about what should be the priorities of a sporting organization. Please tick which ones you think should be the priorities of YOUR organization:

The priorities of MY organization should be to:

Tick ALL that apply:

__ Develop elite performance
__ Improve opportunities for disadvantaged groups (eg: aged, dis-
abled, indigenous people)
__ Create positive role models for ordinary citizens
__ Improve the fitness and health of ordinary citizens
__ Foster international cooperation
__ Build character in children
__ Build national pride
__ Improve opportunities for females
__ Encourage more grass-roots participation
__ Provide more scientific information about training for athletes
and coaches
__ Monitor drug abuse by athletes
__ Develop talented sport administrators
__ Provide first-class facilities for competition
__ Ensure that athletes are adequately prepared for a career after
retiring
__ Other, please specify _____

2. Here are some common statements about organizations. Please tick
the extent of your agreement or disagreement with each statement.

	Strongly Disagree	Disagree	Neither Agree nor Disagree	Agree	Strongly Agree
1. What my organization needs is more women executives	—	—	—	—	—
2. Executives in my organization acquired their positions because they are the best persons for the job	—	—	—	—	—
3. An "inner group" unfairly controls my organization	—	—	—	—	—
4. Women have to work harder than men in my organization to achieve equal recognition	—	—	—	—	—

Questionnaire on the Status of Women Sport Executives

	Strongly Disagree	Disagree	Neither Agree nor Disagree	Agree	Strongly Agree
5. What my organization needs is some strong feminists	—	—	—	—	—
6. Men get ahead more easily than women in my organization	—	—	—	—	—
7. Positions are often advertised after my organization has already identified the persons they want to fill the position	—	—	—	—	—
8. Men treat women as their equals in my organization	—	—	—	—	—
9. Men make better executives than women do in my organization	—	—	—	—	—
10. When being considered for a job in my organization, women are disadvantaged by having family responsibilities	—	—	—	—	—
11. Sexual harassment of women is common in my organization	—	—	—	—	—
12. Women in my organization are too sensitive about jokes concerning females	—	—	—	—	—

	Strongly Disagree	Disagree	Neither Agree nor Disagree	Agree	Strongly Agree
13. Men in my organization have an advantage because they have more role models than women do	—	—	—	—	—
14. The rules of behavior in my organization are much more relaxed for men than for women	—	—	—	—	—
15. Prejudice against gays and/or lesbians is common in my organization	—	—	—	—	—
16. Women in my organization eventually hit a "glass ceiling"	—	—	—	—	—

PART 5: AFFIRMATIVE ACTION ISSUES

1. How effective do you think your organization's affirmative action policies are?

_____

_____

_____

2. Here are some statements about what should be the role of a women's program in sporting organizations. Please tick the extent of your agreement or disagreement with each statement.

The role of a women's program in the organization should be to:

	Strongly Disagree	Disagree	Neither Agree nor Disagree	Agree	Strongly Agree
1. Develop female Executives	—	—	—	—	—

	Strongly Disagree	Disagree	Neither Agree nor Disagree	Agree	Strongly Agree
2. Develop policies and programs specific to females	—	—	—	—	—
3. Raise awareness and understanding of women's issues	—	—	—	—	—
4. Conduct research specific to females	—	—	—	—	—
5. Develop and maintain an effective communication network for females	—	—	—	—	—
6. Monitor and evaluate progress towards the achievement of equality for females	—	—	—	—	—
7. Other, please specify	—	—	—	—	—

4. Here are some reasons often given to explain why women are underrepresented in executive positions in sport. Please tick the extent of your agreement or disagreement with each reason.

	Strongly Disagree	Disagree	Neither Agree nor Disagree	Agree	Strongly Agree
1. The success of informal male networks	—	—	—	—	—
2. Subconscious/ unintentional discrimination by men	—	—	—	—	—
3. The problems women have in travelling or relocating	—	—	—	—	—
4. The constraints of family responsibilities	—	—	—	—	—

175

	Strongly Disagree	Disagree	Neither Agree nor Disagree	Agree	Strongly Agree
5. Lack of women role models	—	—	—	—	—
6. Conscious/intentional discrimination by men	—	—	—	—	—
7. Lack of women with sufficient executive experience	—	—	—	—	—
8. The weakness of informal female networks	—	—	—	—	—
9. Lack of knowledge on the part of women about positions available	—	—	—	—	—
10. Women's lack of commitment	—	—	—	—	—
11. Lack of training opportunities for women	—	—	—	—	—
12. Lack of confidence on the part of women	—	—	—	—	—
13. Lack of commitment by male executives to affirmative action programs	—	—	—	—	—
14. Lack of women mentors	—	—	—	—	—
15. Prejudice against lesbians among executives and staff	—	—	—	—	—
16. Women are not tough enough to cope with executive pressures	—	—	—	—	—

	Strongly Disagree	Disagree	Neither Agree nor Disagree	Agree	Strongly Agree
17. Sexual harass-ment	—	—	—	—	—
18. The "glass ceiling" effect	—	—	—	—	—
19. Other, please explain					
_____	—	—	—	—	—

5. Do you have any other comments you would like to make on:

a. Steps that could or should be taken to remove possible barriers to men or women wishing to advance in sporting organizations? Please continue on the back page if necessary.

_____

_____

_____

_____

_____

b. Affirmative action programs for women executives in sporting organizations? Please continue on the back page if necessary.

_____

_____

_____

_____

_____

_____

_____

This Is the End of the Questionnaire

Appendix 3:
Quantitative Summaries of
Australian Respondents' Perceptions
of Their Organizations

TABLE A.1
Australian Respondents' Perceptions of Why Women Were
Underrepresented in Executive Positions

Reason	Percent Who Agree or Strongly Agree		Percent Who Are Unsure, Disagree, or Strongly Disagree	
	Men	Women	Men	Women
1. Success of informal male networks	30	84	70	16*
2. Subconscious/unintentional discrimination by men	40	77	60	23*
3. Problems women have in travelling/relocating	20	42	80	58*
4. Constraints of family responsibilities	50	91	50	9*
5. Lack of women role models	40	88	60	12*
6. Conscious/intentional discrimination by men	40	44	60	52
7. Lack of women with sufficient executive experience	48	16	52	84*
8. Weakness of informal female networks	25	77	75	23*

Reason	Percent Who Agree or Strongly Agree		Percent Who Are Unsure, Disagree, or Strongly Disagree	
	Men	Women	Men	Women
9. Women's lack of knowledge about positions available	10	16	90	84
10. Women's lack of commitment	5	—	95	100
11. Lack of training opportunities for women	15	65	85	35*
12. Women's lack of confidence	75	85	25	15
13. Male executives' lack of commitment to affirmative action	10	70	90	30*
14. Lack of women mentors	48	83	52	17*
15. Prejudice against lesbians among executives and staff	—	42	100	58*
16. Women not tough enough to cope with executive pressures	10	—	90	100*
17. Sexual harassment	—	42	100	58*

NUMBERS: Men = 40; Women = 43
* Differences significant at .05 level or beyond

TABLE A.2
Australian Respondents' Perceptions of Various Gender Structures
and Processes in Their Organizations

Item	Percent Who Agree or Strongly Agree		Percent Who Are Unsure, Disagree, or Strongly Disagree	
	Men	Women	Men	Women
1. Organization needs more women executives	50	88	50	12*
2. Executives acquired positions because they are the best persons for the job	90	56	10	44*

Australian Respondents' Perceptions of Their Organizations

Item	Percent Who Agree or Strongly Agree		Percent Who Are Unsure, Disagree, or Strongly Disagree	
	Men	Women	Men	Women
3. A strong inner group unfairly controls the organization	52	86	57	14*
4. Women have to work harder than men to achieve equal recognition	53	86	48	14*
5. Organization needs some strong feminists	5	21	95	79
6. Men get ahead more easily than women	57	79	52	21*
7. Positions are often advertised after the organization has already identified whom it wants	—	21	100	79*
8. Men treat women as their equals	95	33	5	67*
9. Men make better executives than women	5	—	95	100
10. When being considered for a job, women are disadvantaged by having family responsibilities	50	86	50	14*
11. Women come up against an invisible barrier once they get to a certain level	25	77	75	23*
12. Sexual harassment of women is common	—	44	100	56*
13. Women are too sensitive about jokes concerning females	43	5	57	95*
14. Men have an advantage because they have more role models than women	40	65	60	35
15. The rules of behavior are much more relaxed for men than for women	10	67	90	33*
16. Prejudice against gays and/or lesbians is common	—	28	100	72*

NUMBERS: Men = 40; Women = 43
* Differences significant at .05 level or beyond

TABLE A.3
Australian Respondents' Perceptions of the Role of a
Women's Committee or Similar Structure in Their Organizations

Reason	Percent Who Agree or Strongly Agree		Percent Who Are Unsure, Disagree, or Strongly Disagree	
	Men	Women	Men	Women
1. To develop female executives	48	81	52	19*
2. To develop policies and programs specific to females	25	67	75	23*
3. To rise awareness and understanding of women's issues	63	81	37	19
4. To conduct research specific to females	13	42	87	58*
5. To develop and maintain an effective communication network for females	15	77	85	23*
6. To monitor and evaluate progress towards the achievement of equality for females	10	47	90	53*

NUMBERS: Men = 40; Women = 43
* Differences significant at .05 level or beyond

Bibliography

ACADEMIC MATERIAL

Acker, J. 1992. "Gendering Organizational Theory." In *Gendering Organizational Analysis*, edited by A. Mills and P. Tancred. London: Sage.

Albo, G., D. Langille, and L. Panitch, eds. 1993. *A Different Kind of State? Popular Power and Democratic Administration*. Toronto: Oxford University Press.

Allan, J. 1991. "When Women Set the Rules." *Canadian Business* 64: 40–43.

Allen, J. 1990. "The Wild Ones: The Disavowal of *Men* in Criminology." In *Dissenting Opinions: Feminist Explorations in Law and Society*, edited by R. Graycar. Sydney: Allen & Unwin.

Ang, I. 1995. "I'm a Feminist But . . . 'Other' Women and Postnational Feminism." In *Transitions: New Australian Feminisms*, edited by B. Caine and R. Pringle. Sydney: Hale & Iremonger.

Antal, A., and D. Izraeli. 1993. "A Global Comparison of Women in Management: Women Managers in Their Homeland and as Expatriates." In *Women in Management*, edited by E. Fagenson. London: Sage.

Armstrong, N. 1992. "Handling the Hydra: Feminist Analyses of the State." In *Feminist Voices: Women's Studies Texts for Aotearoa /*

New Zealand, edited by R. Du Plessis. Melbourne: Oxford University Press.

Bacchi, C. 1993. "The Brick Wall: Why So Few Women Become Academics." *The Australian Universities' Review* 36, 1: 36–41.

Bacchi, C., B. Thiele, J. Eveleine, and J. Currie. 1992. *Shifting Ground: The Dialectics of Work / Care*. Canberra: Research School of Social Sciences, The Australian National University.

Baird, K. 1994. "Attitudes of Australian Women Sports Journalists." *Australian Studies in Journalism* 3: 231–253.

Bell, E., T. Denton, and S. Nkomo. 1993. "Women of Color in Management: Toward an Inclusive Analysis." In *Women in Management*, edited by E. Fagenson. London: Sage.

Bell, M., and L. Hayes. 1994. "From Programming to Partnership: 'Managing' Active Women? National Policy Shifts in the Women in Sport Programmes in Aotearoa/New Zealand." Paper presented at the 10th Commonwealth and International Scientific Congress, Victoria.

Bell, S., and B. Head, eds. 1994. *State, Economy and Public Policy*. Melbourne: Oxford University Press.

Bellamy, P., and K. Ramsay. 1994. *Barriers to Women in Corporate Management*. Report to The Women's Employment, Education and Training Advisory Group. Canberra: Australian Government Publishing Services.

Bennett, J. 1990. "The Secondary School Cheerleader and Ritualized Sexual Exploitation." *The Clearing House* 64: 4–7.

Bennett, R. 1993. "Dismantling the Master's House—A Tale Told in Affirmation of Diversity." *Journal of Health, Physical Education and Recreation* 64: 49–52, 63.

Bennett, T. 1992. "Putting Policy Into Cultural Studies." In *Cultural Studies*, edited by L. Grossberg, C. Nelson, and P. Treichler. London: Routledge.

——— . 1989. "Culture: Theory and Policy." *Culture and Policy* 1: 5–8.

Bennis, W. 1990. *Why Leaders Can't Lead*. Oxford: Jossey-Bass.

Berrett, T. 1993. "The Sponsorship of Amateur Sport—Government, National Sport Organization, and Corporate Perspectives." *Loisir et Sociètè / Society and Leisure* 16: 323–346.

Birrell, S. 1990. "Racial Relations Theories and Sport: Suggestions for a More Critical Analysis." *Sociology of Sport Journal* 6: 212–227.

Birrell, S., and C. Cole. 1990. "Double Fault: Renee Richards and the Construction and Naturalization of Difference." *Sociology of Sport Journal* 7: 1–21.

Birrell, S., and D. Richter. 1987. "Is a Diamond Forever? Feminist Transformations of Sport. *Women's Studies International Forum* 10: 394–409.

Bluckert, P. 1989. "Courage and Spark: Discovering New Meanings and Expressions of Leadership by Men." *Equal Opportunities International* 8, 1: 21–24.

Blum, L., and V. Smith. 1988. "Women's Mobility in the Corporation: A Critique of the Politics of Optimism." *Signs: Journal of Women in Culture and Society* 13: 528–545.

Boston, J., J. Martin, J. Pallot, and P. Walsh, eds. 1991. *Reshaping the State: New Zealand's Bureaucratic Revolution*. Melbourne: Oxford University Press.

Boyle, M., and J. McKay. 1995. "'You Leave Your Troubles at the Gate': A Case Study of the Exploitation of Older Women's Labor and Leisure." *Gender & Society* 9: 556–575.

Bradshaw, J. 1982. "Now What Are They Up To? Men In The 'Men's Movement'." In *On the Problem of Men*, edited by S. Friedman and E. Sarah. London: The Women's Press.

Bredemeier, B. 1992. "'And Ain't I a Woman?' Toward a Multicultural Approach to Gender and Morality." *Quest* 44: 179–209.

Bristow, J. 1988. "How Men Are." *New Formations* 6: 119-131.

Brittan, A. 1989. *Masculinity and Power*. Oxford: Basil Blackwell.

Brod, H., and M. Kimmel, eds. 1994. *Theorizing Masculinities*. London: Sage.

Brown, W. 1992. "Finding the Man in the State." *Feminist Studies* 18, 1: 7–34.

Burroughs, A., L. Ashburn, and L. Seebohn. 1995. "'Add Sex and Stir': Homophobic Coverage of Women's Cricket in Australia." *Journal of Sport and Social Issues* 19: 266–284.

Burt, S. 1993. "The Changing Patterns of Public Policy." In *Changing Patterns: Women in Canada* (2d ed.), edited by S. Burt, L. Code, and L. Dorney. Toronto: McCelland & Stewart.

Burton, C. 1991. *The Promise and the Price. The Struggle for Equal Opportunity in Women's Employment*. Sydney: Allen & Unwin.

Cameron, J. 1996. *Trail Blazers: Women Who Manage New Zealand Sport*. Christchurch, New Zealand: Sport Inclined.

———. 1994. *Women Who Manage: Study of Volunteer National Sports Administrators*. Christchurch, New Zealand: Sociology Department, University of Canterbury.

Canberra Bulletin of Public Administration. 1994. Special Issue on "Women, Organizations and Economic Policies." (no. 76).

Carpenter, L., and V. Acosta. 1991. "Back to the Future: Reform With a Woman's Voice." *Bulletin of the American Association of University Professors* (January/February) 23, 27.

Castles, F. 1989. "Social Protection by Other Means; Australia's Strategy of Coping with External Vulnerability." In *The Comparative History of Public Policy*, edited by F. Castles. Oxford: Polity Press.

Chase, S. 1988. "Making Sense of 'The Woman Who Becomes a Man'." In *Gender and Discourse: The Power of Talk*, edited by A. Todd and S. Fisher. Norwood, N.J.: Ablex.

Clatterbaugh, K. 1992. "The Sexual Oppression Debate in Sexual Politics." In *Rethinking Masculinity: Philosophical Explorations in Light of Feminism*, edited by L. May and R. Strikwerda. Lanham, Md.: Rowman & Littlefield.

Cockburn, C. 1991. *In the Way of Women: Men's Resistance to Sex Equality in Organizations*. London: Macmillan.

Cohn, C. 1987. "Sex and Death in the Rational World of Defense Intellectuals." *Signs* 12: 687–718.

Collins, C., and M. Stuart. 1994. "Politics and Sport in New Zealand." In *Sport Management in New Zealand: An Introduction*, edited by L. Trenberth and C. Collins. Palmerston North, New Zealand: The Dunmore Press.

Collinson, D., and J. Hearn. 1994. "Naming Men as Men: Implications for Work, Organization and Management." *Gender, Work and Organization* 1: 2–22.

Collinson, D., D. Knights, and M. Collinson. 1990. *Managing to Discriminate*. London: Routledge.

Connell, R. W. 1995. *Masculinities*. Sydney: Allen & Unwin.

———. 1993. "The Big Picture: Changing Masculinities in the Perspective of Recent World History." *Theory and Society* 22: 597–623.

———. 1992. "Drumming up the Wrong Tree." *Tikkun* 7, 1: 31–36.

———. 1990a. "The State, Gender and Sexual Politics: Theory and Appraisal." *Theory and Society* 19: 507–544.

———. 1990b. "An Iron Man: The Body and Some Contradictions of Hegemonic Masculinity." In *Sport, Men, and the Gender Order: Critical Feminist Perspectives*, edited by M. Messner and D. Sabo. Champaign, Ill.: Human Kinetics Press.

———. 1987. *Gender and Power*. Sydney: Allen & Unwin.

———. 1983. *Which Way Is Up?* Sydney: George Allen & Unwin.

Coser, L. 1974. *Greedy Institutions: Patterns of Undivided Commitment*. New York: Free Press.

Crompton, R., and N. Le Feuvre. 1992. "Gender and Bureaucracy: Women in Finance in Britain and France." In *Gender and Bureaucracy*, edited by M. Savage and A. Witz. Oxford: Blackwell.

Crossett, T., J. Benedict, and M. McDonald. 1995. "Male Student-athletes Reported for Sexual Assault: A Survey of Campus Police

Departments and Judicial Affairs Offices." *Journal of Sport and Social Issues* 19: 126–140.

Cunningham, S. 1992. *Framing Culture: Criticism and Policy in Australia.* Sydney: Allen & Unwin.

Curry, T. 1991. "Fraternal Bonding in the Locker Room: A Profeminist Analysis of Talk About Competition and Women." *Sociology of Sport Journal* 8: 119–135.

Davidson, M., and C. Cooper, eds. 1994. *Women in Management: Current Research Issues.* London: Paul Chapman.

———. 1992. *Shattering the Glass Ceiling: The Woman Manager.* London: Paul Chapman.

Davis, L. 1990. "Male Cheerleaders and the Naturalization of Gender." In *Sport, Men, and the Gender Order: Critical Feminist Perspectives*, edited by M. Messner and D. Sabo. Champaign, Ill.: Human Kinetics Press.

Davis, N. 1994. "Teaching About Inequality: Student Resistance, Paralysis, and Rage." *Teaching Sociology* 20: 232–238.

Douglas, P. 1994. "'New Men' and the Tensions of Profeminism." *Social Alternatives* 12: 33–35

Dowse, S. 1988. "The Women's Movement Fandango With the State: The Movement's Role in Public Policy Since 1972." In *Women, Social Welfare and the State* (2d ed.), edited by C. Baldock and B. Cass. Sydney: Allen & Unwin.

Duelli Klein, R. 1983. "The 'Men-Problem' in Women's Studies: The Expert, the Ignoramus and the Poor Dear." *Women's Studies International Forum* 6: 413–421.

du Gay, P. 1991. "Enterprise Culture and the Ideology of Excellence." *New Formations* 13: 45–61.

Dunk, T. 1991. *It's a Working Man's Town: Male Working-Class Culture in Northwestern Ontario.* Montreal: McGill-Queen's University Press.

Du Plessis, R. 1995. "Women in a Restructured New Zealand: Lessons for Australia." In *Women in a Restructuring Australia*, edited by A. Edwards and S. Magarey. Sydney: Allen & Unwin.

————. 1992. "Stating the Contradictions: The Case of Women's Employment." In *Feminist Voices: Women's Studies Texts for Aotearoa/New Zealand*, edited by R. Du Plessis. Melbourne: Oxford University Press.

Eberhard, W., and M. Myers. 1988. "Beyond the Locker Room: Women in Sports on Major Daily Newspapers." *Journalism Quarterly* 65: 595–599.

Ebert, T. 1992–93. "Ludic Feminism, the Body, Performance, and Labor: Bringing *Materialism* Back Into Feminist Cultural Studies." *Cultural Critique* 23: 5–50.

Edgar, D. 1991. Foreword to *Work and Family: Employer's Views* by I. Wolcott. Melbourne: Australian Institute of Family Studies.

Eisenstein, H. 1991. *Gender Shock: Practising Feminism on Two Continents*. Sydney: Allen & Unwin.

Else, A. 1992. "To Market and Home Again: Gender and the New Right." In *Feminist Voices: Women's Studies Texts for Aotearoa/New Zealand*, edited by R. Du Plessis. Melbourne: Oxford University Press.

Epstein, C. 1992. "Tinkerbells and Pinups: The Construction of Gender Boundaries at Work." In *Cultivating Difference: Symbolic Boundaries and the Marking of Inequality*, edited by M. Lamont and M. Fournier. Chicago: University of Chicago Press.

————. 1991. "Ways Men and Women Lead." *Harvard Business Review* (January/February) 150–151.

Fagenson, E., ed. 1993. *Women in Management*. London: Sage.

Fasting, K. 1987. "The Promotion of Women's Involvement in Norwegian Sports Organizations." In *The Organization and Administration of Sport*, edited by T. Slack and R. Hinings. London: Sports Dynamics Publishers.

Fasting, K., and M. K. Sisjord. 1986. "Gender, Verbal Behaviour and Power in Sports Organisations." *Scandinavian Journal of Sports Science* 8: 81–85.

Foley, J. 1990. "The Great American Football Ritual: Reproducing Race, Class, and Gender Inequality." *Sociology of Sport Journal* 7: 111–135.

Franklin, S., C. Lury, and J. Stacey, eds. 1991. *Off-centre: Feminism and Cultural Studies*. London: Harper Collins.

Franzway, S., D. Court, and R. W. Connell, eds. 1989. *Staking a Claim: Feminism, Bureaucracy and the State*. Sydney: Allen & Unwin.

Freeman, S. 1990. *Managing Lives: Corporate Women and Social Change*. Amherst: University of Massachusetts Press.

Fritner, M. P., and L. Rubinson. 1993. "Acquaintance Rape: The Influence of Alcohol, Fraternity Membership, and Sports Team Membership." *Journal of Sex Education and Therapy* 4: 272–284.

Game, A., and R. Pringle. 1986. *Gender at Work*. Sydney: Allen & Unwin.

Gatens, M. 1992. "Power, Bodies and Difference." In *Destabilizing Theory: Contemporary Feminist Debates*, edited by M. Barrett and A. Phillips. Oxford: Polity Press.

Gibson, J. W. 1994. *Warrior Dreams: Paramilitary Culture in Post-Vietnam America*. New York: Hill and Wang.

Gidlow, B., G. Cushman, and H. Perkins. 1995. "Whatever Happened to 'Recreation'? Changes in New Zealand State Leisure Policy." *Australian and New Zealand Association for Leisure Research Series*, Vol. 2: 76–93.

Goode, W. 1992. "Why Men Resist." In *Rethinking The Family: Some Feminist Questions* (2d ed.), edited by B. Thorne & M. Yalom. London: Longman.

Grant, J., and P. Porter. 1994. "Women Managers: The Construction of Gender in the Work Place." *Australian and New Zealand Journal of Sociology* 30, 2: 149–164.

Griffin, P. 1992. "Changing the Game: Homophobia, Sexism, and Lesbians in Sport." *Quest* 44: 251–265.

————. 1991. "From Hiding Out To Coming Out: Empowering Lesbian and Gay Educators." *Journal of Homosexuality* 22, 3/4: 167–212.

Gruneau, R., and D. Whitson. 1994. *Hockey Night in Canada: Sport, Identities and Cultural Politics*. Toronto: Garamond Press.

Hall, E. 1993. "Waitering/Waitressing: Engendering the Work of Table Servers." *Gender & Society* 7: 329–346.

Hall, M. A. 1996. *Feminism and Sporting Bodies: Essays in Theory and Practice*. Champaign, Ill.: Human Kinetics Press.

————. 1995. "Women in Sport: From Liberal Activism to Radical Cultural Struggle." In *Changing Methods: Feminists Transforming Practice*, edited by L. Code and S. Burt. Toronto: Broadview Press.

————. 1994. "Women's Sport Advocacy Organizations: Comparing Feminist Activism in Sport." *Journal of Comparative Physical Education and Sport* 16: 50–59.

Hall, M. A., D. Cullen, and T. Slack. 1990. "The Gender Structure of National Sport Organisations." *Sport Canada Occasional Papers*. Vol. 2, No. 1.

————. 1989. "Organizational Elites Recreating Themselves: The Gender Structure of National Sports Organizations." *Quest* 41: 28–45.

Hall, M. A., T. Slack, G. Smith, and D. Whitson. 1991. *Sport in Canadian Society*. Toronto: McClelland & Stewart.

Hall, S. 1985. "Signification, Representation, Ideology: Althusser and the Post-structuralist Debates." *Critical Studies in Mass Communication* 2, 2: 91–114.

Harvey, J., L. Thibault, and G. Rail. 1995. "Neo-corporatism: The Political Management System in Canadian Amateur Sport and Fitness." *Journal of Sport and Social Issues* 19: 249–265.

Hearn, J. 1994. "Changing Men and Changing Managements: Social Change, Social Research and Social Action." In *Women in Management: Current Research Issues*, edited by M. Davidson and C. Cooper. London: Paul Chapman.

———. 1992. "Changing Men and Changing Managements: A Review of Issues and Actions." *Women in Management Review* 7, 1: 3–8.

———. 1989. "Leading Questions for Men's Leadership, Feminist Challenges, and Men's Responses." *Equal Opportunities International* 8, 1: 3–11.

Hearn, J., and W. Parkin. 1987. *Sex at Work*. Brighton, England: Wheatsheaf.

Hearn, J., D. Sheppard, P. Tancred-Sheriff, and P. Burrell, eds. 1990. *The Sexuality of Organisation*. London: Sage.

Heath, S. 1986. "Male Feminism." *Dalhousie Review* 64: 270-301.

Herdt, G., ed. 1994. *Third Sex, Third Gender: Beyond Sexual Dimorphism in Culture and History*. New York: Zone Books.

Hester, M. 1984. "Anti-sexist Men: A Case of Cloak-and-Dagger Chauvinism." *Women's Studies International Forum* 7: 33–37.

Hewitson, G. 1994. "Neo-classical Economics: A Feminist Perspective." In *Australian Women: Contemporary Feminist Thought*, edited by N. Grieve and A. Burns. Melbourne: Oxford University Press.

Hindson, A., G. Cushman, and B. Gidlow. 1994. "Historical and Social Perspectives on Sport in New Zealand." In *Sport Management in New Zealand: An Introduction*, edited by L. Trenberth and C. Collins. Palmerston North, New Zealand: The Dunmore Press.

Holloway, W. 1994. "Separation, Integration and Difference: Contradictions in a Gender Regime." In *Power/Gender: Social Relations in Theory and Practice*, edited by H. Radke and H. Stam. London: Sage.

Hood, C. 1995. "The 'New Public Management' in the 1980s: Variations on a Theme." *Accounting, Organizations and Society* 20, 2/3: 93–109.

hooks, b. 1984. *Feminist Theory: From Margin to Center*. Boston: South End Press.

Hughes, R., and J. Coakley. 1991. "Positive Deviance Among Athletes: The Implications of Overconformity to the Sport Ethic." *Sociology of Sport Journal* 8: 61–69.

Hyman, P. 1994. "New Zealand Since 1984: Economic Restructuring—Feminist Response, Activity and Theory." *Hecate* 20, 2: 9–35.

———. 1992. "The Use of Economic Orthodoxy to Justify Inequality: A Feminist Critique." In *Feminist Voices: Women's Studies Texts for Aotearoa / New Zealand*, edited by R. Du Plessis. Melbourne: Oxford University Press.

Iannello, K. 1992. *Decisions Without Hierarchy: Feminist Interventions in Organizations Theory and Practice*. London: Routledge.

Jackson, S. 1992. "The Amazing Deconstructing Woman." *Trouble & Strife* 25: 25–31.

James, B., and K. Saville-Smith. 1992. "The 'Invisible Woman' in Organisational Theory." In *The Gender Factor: Women in New Zealand Organisations*, edited by S. Olsson. Palmerston North, New Zealand: The Dunmore Press.

Jeffords, S. 1994. *Hard Bodies: Hollywood Masculinity in the Reagan Era*. New Brunswick: Rutgers University Press.

———. 1989. *The Remasculinization of America: Gender and the Vietnam War*. Bloomington: University of Indiana Press.

Johnson, A. S. McBride, and P. Smith, eds. 1994. *Continuities and Discontinuities: The Political Economy of Social Welfare and Labour Market Policy in Canada*. Toronto: University of Toronto Press.

Johnson, C. 1993. "'Fightback' and Masculine Identity: A Postscript on the 1993 Election." *Australian Feminist Studies* 17: 81–93.

Kandiyoti, D. 1988. "Bargaining with Patriarchy." *Gender & Society* 2: 274–290.

Kane, M. J. 1995. "Resistance/Transformation of the Oppositional Binary: Exposing Sport as a Continuum." *Journal of Sport and Social Issues* 19: 191–218.

Kane, M. J., and L. Disch. 1993. "Sexual Violence and the Reproduction of Male Power in the Locker Room: A Critical Analysis of the 'Lisa Olson Incident'." *Sociology of Sport Journal* 10: 331–352.

Kanter, R. 1977. *Men and Women of the Corporation*. New York: Basic Books.

Karpin, D. 1995. *Enterprising Nation: Renewing Australia's Managers to Meet the Challenges of the Asian-Pacific Century.* Canberra: Australian Government Publishing Service.

Katz, J. 1995. "Reconstructing Masculinity in the Locker Room: The Mentors in Violence Project." *Harvard Educational Review* 65: 163–174.

Keat, R., and N. Abercrombie, eds. 1990. *Enterprise Culture*. London: Routledge.

Kelsey, J. 1993. *Rolling Back the State: Privatisation of Power in Aotearoa/New Zealand*. Wellington: Bridget Williams Books.

Kenway, J. 1995. "Masculinities in Schools: Under Siege, on the Defensive and Under Reconstruction?" *Discourse: Studies in the Cultural Politics of Education* 16: 59–79.

———. 1992. "Feminist Theories of the State: To be or not to be?" In *Society, State and Politics in Australia*, edited by M. Muetzelfeldt. Sydney: Pluto.

Kerfoot, D., and D. Knights. 1993. "Management, Masculinity and Manipulation: From Paternalism to Corporate Strategy in Financial Services in Britain." *Journal of Management Studies* 30: 660–677.

Kidd, B. 1995. "Inequality in Sport, the Corporation, and the State: An Agenda for Social Scientists." *Journal of Sport and Social Issues* 19: 232–248.

———. 1988. "The Philosophy of Excellence: Olympic Performance, Class Power, and the Canadian State." In *Philosophy of Sport and Physical Activity*, edited by P. Galasso. Toronto: Canadian Scholars Press.

Kikulius, L., T. Slack, and B. Hinings. 1992. "Institutionally Specific Design Archetypes: A Framework for Understanding Change in National Sport Organizations." *International Review for the Sociology of Sport* 27: 343–369.

Kimmel, M. 1993. "Invisible Masculinity." *Society* September/October, 28–35.

———. 1992. *Against the Tide: Pro-feminist Men in the United States 1776–1990. A Documentary History*. Boston: Beacon.

Kimmel, M., and M. Messner, eds. 1995. *Men's Lives* (3d ed.). New York: Macmillan.

Klein, A. 1995. "Tender Machos: Masculine Contrasts in the Mexican Baseball League." *Sociology of Sport Journal* 12: 370–388.

———. 1993. *Little Big Men: Bodybuilding, Subculture, and Gender Construction*. Albany: State University of New York Press.

Knoppers, A. 1992. "Explaining Male Dominance and Sex Segregation in Coaching: Three Approaches." *Quest* 44: 210–227.

Koss, M., and J. Gaines. 1993. "The Prediction of Aggression by Alcohol Use, Athletic Participation, and Fraternity Affiliation." *Journal of Interpersonal Violence* 8: 94–108.

Krenske, L. 1993. "Boys Keep Swinging: The Social Construction and Corporeality and Gender Differences in Heavy Metal Music." Honours Thesis, Department of Anthropology and Sociology, The University of Queensland.

Larner, W. 1993. "Changing Contexts: Globalization, Migration and Feminism in New Zealand." In *Feminism and the Politics of Difference*, edited by A. Gunew and A. Yeatman. Sydney: Allen & Unwin.

LaRossa, R. 1995. "Fatherhood and Social Change. In *Men's Lives* (3d ed.), edited by M. Kimmel and M. Messner. Boston: Allyn and Bacon.

Legge, K. 1987. "Women in Personnel Management: Uphill Climb or Downhill Slide?" In *In a Man's World: Essays on Women in Male-Dominated Professions*, edited by A. Spencer and D. Podmore. London: Tavistock.

Lenskyj, H. 1993. "False Starts: System Responses to Violence Against Women." Paper presented at the National Girls and Women in Sport Symposium, Slippery Rock, Penn., February 22–29.

――― . 1992a. "Unsafe at Home Base: Women's Experiences of Sexual Harassment in University Sport and Physical Education." *Women in Sport and Physical Activity Journal* 1: 19–33.

――― . 1992b. "Sexual Harassment: Female Athletes' Experiences and Coaches Responsibilities. *Science Periodical on Research and Technology in Sport* 12, 6: 1–5.

――― . 1991. "Combating Homophobia in Sport and Physical Education." *Sociology of Sport Journal* 8: 61–69.

Liff, S., and J. Wajcman. 1995. "'Sameness' and 'Difference' Revisited: Which Way Forward for Equal Opportunity Initiatives?" *Journal of Management Studies* 33: 79–84.

Lorber, J., and S. A. Farrell, eds. 1991. *The Social Construction of Gender*. London: Sage.

Lorde, A. 1979. *Sister Outsider: Essays and Speeches by Audre Lorde*. Freedom, Cal.: The Crossing Press.

Lupiano, D. 1994. "Equity in Women's Sports: A Health and Fairness Perspective." *Clinics in Sports Medicine* 13, 2: 281–296.

Lynch, L. 1984. "Bureaucratic Feminisms: Bossism and Beige Suits." *Refractory Girl* 27: 38–44.

Macintosh, D., and D. Whitson. 1990. *The Game Planners: Transforming Canada's Sport System*. Montreal and Kingston: McGill-Queens University Press.

MacKinnon, C. 1987. *Feminism Unmodified*. Cambridge: Harvard University Press.

Maier, M. 1992. "Evolving Paradigms of Management in Organizations: A Gendered Analysis." *Journal of Management Systems* 4, 1: 29–42.

Marshall, J. 1984. *Women Managers: Travellers in a Male World*. Chichester, England: Wiley.

Martin, L. 1994. "Power, Continuity and Change: Decoding Black and White Women Managers' Experience in Local Government." In *Women in Management: A Developing Presence*, edited by M. Tanton. London: Routledge.

Martin, P. 1993. "Feminist Practice in Organizations: Implications for Management." In *Women in Management*, edited by E. Fagenson. London: Sage.

McBride, J. 1995. *War, Battering, and Other Sports. The Gulf Between American Men and Women*. Atlantic Heights, N.J.: Humanities Press.

McBride, S., and J. Shields. 1993. *Dismantling a Nation: Canada and the New World Order*. Halifax: Fernwood.

McDowell, L., and G. Court. 1994. "Performing Work: Bodily Representations in Merchant Banks." *Society and Space* 12: 727–750.

McGregor, J., M. Thomson, and P. Dewe. 1994. *Women in Management in New Zealand: A Benchmark Survey*. Women in Management Series, Paper No. 19. Nepean: Faculty of Commerce, University of Western Sydney.

McKay, J. 1995. "'Just Do It': Corporate Sports Slogans and the Political Economy of 'Enlightened Racism'." *Discourse: Studies in the Cultural Politics of Education* 16: 191–201.

———. 1993. "'Marked Men' and 'Wanton Women': The Politics of Naming Sexual 'Deviance' in Sport." *The Journal of Men's Studies* 2, 1: 69–87.

———. 1992a. *Why So Few? Women Executives in Australian Sport*. Belconnen, Australia: Australian Sports Commission.

———. 1992b. "Sport and the Social Construction of Gender." In *Society and Gender: An Introduction to Sociology*, edited by G. Lupton, T. Short, and R. Whip. Sydney: Macmillan.

———. 1991. *No Pain, No Gain? Sport and Australian Culture*. Sydney: Prentice Hall.

McKay, J., and D. Huber. 1992. "Anchoring Images of Technology and Sport." *Women's Studies International Forum* 15: 205-218.

McKay, J., G. Lawrence, T. Miller, and D. Rowe. 1993. Globalization, Postmodernism and Australian Sport, *Sport Science Review* 2, 1: 10–28.

McKay, J., and I. Middlemiss. 1995. "'Mate Against Mate, State Against State': A Case Study of Media Constructions of Hegemonic Masculinity in Australian Sport." *Masculinities* 3, 3: 38-47.

McKay, J., and E. Ogilvie. (in press). "New Age—Same Old Men: Constructing the 'New Man' in the Australian Media." *Mattoid*.

McKay, J., and P. Smith. 1995. "Exonerating the Hero: Frames and Narratives in Media Coverage of the O.J. Simpson Story." *Media Information Australia* 75: 57–66.

McKeganey, N., and M. Bloor. 1991. "Spotting the Invisible Man: The Influence of Male Gender on Fieldwork Relations." *British Journal of Sociology* 42: 195–209.

Melnick, M. 1992. "Male Athletes and Sexual Assault." *Journal of Health, Physical Education and Recreation* 63: 32–35.

Messner, M. 1997. *Politics of Masculinities: Men in Movements*. Thousand Oaks, Cal.: Sage.

———. 1996. "Studying Up On Sex." *Sociology of Sport Journal* 13: 221–238.

———. 1990a. "When Bodies are Weapons: Masculinity and Violence in Sport. *International Review for the Sociology of Sport* 25: 203–219.

———. 1990b. "Men Studying Masculinity: Some Epistemological Issues in Sport Sociology." *Sociology of Sport Journal* 7: 136-153.

Messner, M., M. C. Duncan, and K. Jensen. 1994. "Separating the Men From the Girls: The Gendered Language of Televised Sports." *Gender & Society* 7: 121–137.

Messner M., and D. Sabo. 1994. *Sex, Violence and Power in Sports: Rethinking Masculinity*. Freedom, Cal.: The Crossing Press.

Miller, P., and N. Rose. 1994. "Governing Economic Life." *Economy and Society* 19: 1–31.

Morgan, D. 1981. "Men, Masculinity and the Process
    Enquiry." In *Doing Feminist Research*, edited b
    London: Routledge.

Morgan, G. 1986. *Images of Organizations*. New York

Morrison, A., R. White, and E. Van Velsor. 1987. *Brea*
    Ceiling. New York: Addison-Wesley.

Morse, M. 1983. "Sport on Television: Replay an
    Regarding Television, edited by A. Kaplan. Freder

Mouzelis, N. 1993. "The Poverty of Sociological Theory
    675–695.

Nauright, J., ed. 1995. *Sport, Power and Society in*
    Sydney: Australian Society for Sports History.

Overall, C. 1987. "Role Models: A Critique." In *Women*
    Bondings, edited by K. Storrie. Toronto: Cana
    Institute for the Advancement of Women.

Padavic, I. 1991. "The Re-creation of Gender in a Ma
    Symbolic Interaction 14: 279–294.

Pateman, C. 1988. "The Patriarchal Welfare State."
    and the Welfare State, edited by H. Gutmar
    Princeton University Press.

Perkins, H., P. Devlin, D. Simmons, and R. Batty. 19!
    and Tourism." In *Environmental Planning in*
    edited by P. Memon and H. Perkins. Palmerston
    The Dunmore Press.

Pfiel, F. 1995. *White Guys*. London: Verso.

Phillips, J. 1987. *A Man's Country? The Image of the*
    History. Auckland: Penguin.

Poiner, G., and S. Wills. 1991. *The Gifthorse. A Critica*
    Opportunity in Australia. Sydney: Allen & Unv

Powell, G. 1993. *Women and Men in Management* (2
    Sage.

———. 1988. *Women and Men in Management*. Lon

BIBLIOGRAPHY

gle, R. 1988. *Secretaries Talk: Sexuality, Power & Work*. Sydney: Allen & Unwin.

gle, R., and S. Watson. 1992. "Women's Interests and the Post-structuralist State." In *Destabilizing Theory: Contemporary Feminist Debates*, edited by M. Barrett and A. Phillips. Oxford: Polity Press.

ger, B. 1991. *The Arena of Masculinity*. New York: St. Martins Press.

y, M. 1991. *Economic Rationalism in Canberra: A Nation-building State Changes its Mind*. London: Cambridge University Press.

ord Ruether, R. 1993. "Patriarchy and the Men's Movement: Part of the Problem or Part of the Solution?" In *Women Respond to the Men's Movement*, edited by K. Hagan. San Francisco: Pandora.

io, M. R. 1986. "The Life and Careers of Women in Leading Positions in Finnish Sports Organisations." In *Sport, Culture, Society: International Perspectives*, edited by J. Mangan and R. Small. London: E. & F. Spon.

, S. 1994. "Economic Rationalism: An Ideology of Exclusion." *Australian Quarterly* 29: 171–185.

in, B., and P. Roos. 1990. *Job Queues, Gender Queues: Women's Inroads Into Male Occupations*. Philadelphia: Temple University Press.

rdson, D., and V. Robinson. 1994. "Theorizing Women's Studies, Gender Studies and Masculinity: The Politics of Naming." *The European Journal of Women's Studies* 1: 11-27.

r, M. 1994. *The British Organizational Man Since 1945*. Oxford: Oxford University Press.

, S. 1989. "Leadership, Men and Equality." *Equal Opportunities International* 8, 1: 25–28.

D., and S. Jansen. 1992. "Images of Men in Sport Media: The Social Reproduction of the Gender Order." In *Men, Masculinity, and the Media*, edited by S. Craig. Sage, London.

Sanday, P. 1981. *Female Power and Male Dominance: On the Origins of Sexual Inequality*. Cambridge: Cambridge University Press.

Sawer, M. 1994. "Feminism and the State: Theory and Practice in Australia and Canada." *Australian-Canadian Studies* 12: 49–69.

Schein, V. 1994. "Managerial Sex Typing: A Persistent and Pervasive Barrier to Women's Opportunities." In *Women in Management: Current Research Issues*, edited by M. Davidson and C. Cooper. London: Paul Chapman.

Semotiuk, D. 1994. "Restructuring Canada's National Sports System: The Legacy of the Dubin Inquiry." In *Sport in the Global Village*, edited by R. Wilcox. Morgantown, W.V.: Fitness Information Technology.

Shaver, S. 1990. "Gender, Social Policy Regimes and the Welfare State." The University of New South Wales Social Policy Research Centre. Discussion Paper No. 26.

Simmons, M. 1989. "Creating a New Men's Leadership: Developing a Theory and Practice." *Equal Opportunities International* 8, 1: 16–20.

Sinclair, A. 1994. *Trials at the Top*. Melbourne: The Australian Centre, The University of Melbourne.

Slack, T., and B. Hinings. 1994. "Institutional Pressures and Isomorphic Change: An Empirical Test." *Organization Studies* 15: 803–827.

Smith, Y. 1992. "Women of Color in Sport." *Quest* 44: 228–250.

Spender, D. 1981. *Men's Studies Modified: The Impact of Feminism on the Academic Disciplines*. Oxford: Pergamon Press.

Starhawk. 1993. "A Men's Movement I Can Trust." In *Women Respond to the Men's Movement*, edited by K. Hagan. San Francisco: Pandora.

Steinberg, R. 1992. "Gender on the Agenda: Male Advantage in Organizations." *Contemporary Sociology* 21: 576–581.

Still, L. 1993. *Where to from Here? The Managerial Woman in Transition*. Sydney: Business & Professional Publishing.

Stolcke, V. 1981. "Women's Labours: The Naturalisation of Social Inequality and Women's Subordination." In *Of Marriage and the Market*, edited by K. Young, C. Wolkowitz, and R. McCullogh. London: CSE Books.

Tanton, M., ed. 1994. *Women in Management: A Developing Presence*. London: Routledge.

Theberge, N. 1987. "Sport and Women's Empowerment." *Women's Studies International Forum* 10: 387–393.

Thompson, S. 1992. "'Mum's Tennis Day': The Gendered Definition of Older Women's Leisure." *Loisir et Sociètè / Society and Leisure* 15: 271–289.

———. "'Mum's Taxi': Gendered Servicing of Sport." Paper presented at The Australian Sociological Association annual conference. Perth: Murdoch University, 10–14 December.

———. 1990. "'Thank the Ladies for the Plates': The Incorporation of Women into Sport." *Leisure Studies* 9: 135–143.

Thornton, M. 1994. "The Seductive Allure of EEO." In *Australian Women: Contemporary Feminist Thought*, edited by N. Grieve and A. Burns. Melbourne: Oxford University Press.

Trujillo, N. 1995. "Machines, Missiles, and Men: Images of the Male Body on ABC's *Monday Night Football*." *Sociology of Sport Journal* 12: 403–423.

———. 1991. "Hegemonic Masculinity on the Mound: Media Representations of Nolan Ryan and American Sports Culture." *Critical Studies in Mass Communication* 8: 290–308.

Vilkinas, T. 1991. "Australian Women in Management." *Women in Management Review* 6: 17–21.

Volkerling, J. 1994. "Death or Transfiguration: The Future for Cultural Policy in New Zealand." *Culture and Policy* 6, 1: 7–28.

Walby, S. 1992. "Post-Post-Modern? Theorizing Social Complexity." In *Destabilizing Theory: Contemporary Feminist Debates*, edited by M. Barrett and A. Phillips. Oxford: Polity Press.

Wark, M. 1992. "After Literature: Culture, Policy, Theory and Beyond." *Meanjin* 51, 4: 677–690.

Watson, S. 1992. "Femocratic Feminisms." In *Gender and Bureaucracy*, edited by M. Savage and A. Witz. Oxford: Blackwell.

Watson, S., ed. 1991. *Playing the State. Australian Feminist Interventions*. Sydney: Allen & Unwin.

Weeks, J. 1985. *Sexuality and its Discontents: Meanings, Myths and Modern Sexualities*. London: Routledge & Kegan Paul.

West, A., and C. Brackenridge. 1990. *Wot! No Women Sports Coaches? A Report on the Issues Relating to Women's Lives as Sports Coaches in the United Kingdom: 1989 / 1990*. Sheffield City Polytechnic: PAVIC Publications.

West, C. 1989. "Black Culture and Postmodernism." In *Remaking History*, edited by B. Kruger and P. Mariani. Seattle: Bay Press.

West, C., and D. Zimmerman. 1987. "Doing Gender." *Gender & Society* 1: 125–151.

White, A., and C. Brackenridge. 1985. "Who Rules Sport? Gender Divisions in the Power Structure of British Sports Organisations From 1960." *International Review for the Sociology of Sport* 20: 96–107.

White, A., R. Mayglothing, and C. Carr. 1991. *The Dedicated Few— The Social World of Women Coaches in Britain in the 1990s*. West Sussex Institute of Higher Education: Centre for the Study and Promotion of Sport and Recreation for Women and Girls.

White, G., J. Katz, and K. Scarborough. 1992. "The Impact of Professional Football Games Upon Violent Assaults on Women." *Violence and Victims* 7: 157–171.

Whitson, D., and D. Macintosh. 1990. "Equity vs. High Performance in Canadian Amateur Sport." *CAHPER Journal* May/June, 27–30.

Wieneke, C. 1992. "Does Equal Employment Opportunity Serve the Women's Movement? A Case Study from Australian Higher Education." In *Working Out: New Directions for Women's Studies*, edited by H. Hinds, A. Phoenis, and J. Stacey. London: The Falmer Press.

——— . 1991. "Equal Employment Opportunity in Australia: A Practitioner's Perspective." *Equal Opportunity International* 10, 1: 1–10.

Wieneke, C., and M. Durham. 1992. "Regulating the Equality Agenda: EEO in Higher Education." *Australian Universities Review* 35, 2: 30–35.

Williams, C. 1995. *Still a Man's World: Men Who Do Women's Work*. Berkeley: University of California Press.

Williams, C., and E. Heikes. 1993. "The Importance of Gender in the In-depth Interview." *Gender & Society* 7: 280–291.

Williams, J., and R. Taylor. 1994. "Boys Keep Swinging: Masculinity and Football Culture in England." In *Just Boys Doing Business? Men, Masculinities and Crime*, T. Newburn and E. Stanko, eds. London: Routledge.

Willmott, H., 1993. "Strength is Ignorance; Slavery is Freedom: Managing Culture in Modern Organizations." *Journal of Management Studies* 30: 515–552.

Winter, M., and E. Robert. 1980. "Male Dominance, Late Capitalism, and the Growth of Instrumental Reason." *Berkeley Journal of Sociology* 24: 249–280.

Wise, S., and L. Stanley. 1984. "Sexual Sexual Politics." *Women's Studies International Forum* 7: 1–6.

Witz, A. 1990. "Patriarchy and Professions: The Gendered Politics of Occupational Closure." *Sociology* 24: 675–690.

Woldring, K. 1996. "The Concrete Ceiling: A Sympathetic View of a Waste of Talent." *Policy, Organization & Society* 11: 111–127.

Yeatman, A. 1994. "Women and the State." In *Contemporary Australian Feminism*, edited by K. Pritchard Hughes. Melbourne: Longman Chesire.

——— . 1990. *Bureaucrats, Technocrats, Femocrats: Essays on the Contemporary Australian State*. Sydney: Allen & Unwin.

Young, I. 1990. *Justice and the Politics of Difference*. Princeton: Princeton University Press.

GOVERNMENT AND RELATED DOCUMENTS

Australian Sports Commission. 1992. *Facts Sheets*. Belconnen.

―――. 1991a. *Towards Equity in Sport*. Belconnen.

―――. 1991b. *Proceedings of the Sportswomen Step Forward Conference*. Belconnen.

―――. 1987. *Sport to the Year 2000*. Canberra.

Heylen Research Centre. 1994. *Examining Client Relationships*. Wellington: Heylen Research Centre.

Hillary Commission for Recreation and Sport. 1993. *Annual Report*. Wellington: Hillary Commission for Sport, Fitness and Leisure.

―――. 1992. *Annual Report*. Wellington: Hillary Commission for Sport, Fitness and Leisure.

―――. 1988. *First Annual Report*. Wellington.

House of Representatives Standing Committee on Legal and Constitutional Affairs. 1992. *Half Way to Equal*. Report of the Inquiry Into Equal Status and Equal Opportunity for Women in Australia. Canberra.

―――. 1991. *Equity for Women in Sport*. Canberra.

Ministry of Supply and Services. 1991. *Beneath the Veneer: The Report of the Task Force on Barriers to Women in The Public Service*. Ottawa: Canadian Government Publishing Service.

Punch, G. 1988. "Speech in the House of Representatives." *Daily Hansard*, 31 August, 725–729.

Timpson, M. 1991. "Public Policy and Funding of Women's Sport." In *Equity for Women in Sport*. Canberra: House of Representatives Standing Committee on Legal and Constitutional Affairs.

NEWSPAPER, MAGAZINE AND MISCELLANEOUS ARTICLES

Bagwell, S. "It's A Man's Games Isn't It?" *The Australian Financial Review*, September, 29, 1993, 17.

Bentley, D. "Origin War Fought In Footy Pig Pen." *The Sunday Sun*, June 9, 1991, 45.

Carruthers, F. 1997. "Women Lose Battle of the Boardrooms." *The Weekend Australian*, February 8–9, 1, 6.

Ellicot, J. 1997. "Socialite Wins Olympic PR Job." *The Australian*, February 6, 3.

Kavanagh, L. "Women Athletes Just Don't Pack 'Em In Like Men." *The Courier-Mail*, March 19, 1990, 8.

Macdonald, J. "Off The Beat." *The Sydney Morning Herald*, March 9, 1991, 76.

Magnay, J. "Best For Less." *The Sydney Morning Herald*, August 2, 1995, 11.

Malone, P. "Get The Courier Femail, You Can't Beat It For The Best Sport Of All." *The Courier-Mail*, March 24, 1990, 86.

Mandle, B. "Flaunt it, Athletes, But Cop the Result." *The Canberra Times*, January 31, 1990, 6.

Masters, R. "Masters." *The Sydney Morning Herald*, November 21, 1993, 78.

——— . "If You've Got It, Flaunt It, Be Ye A He Or A She." *The Sydney Morning Herald*, March 5, 1991, 74.

Miranda, C. "Report Fails To Address Its Principle Concern." *The Canberra Times*, February 26, 1993, 26.

Moore, M. 1997. "City Socialite To Be The New Face Of SOCOG." *The Sydney Morning Herald*, February 6, 6.

Rowe, D. "Hold The Back Page For *The* Sporting Challenge." *The Sydney Morning Herald*, July 18, 1990, 11.

Smart, G. "Sport Sexism Is Nonsense." *The Sunday Mail*, March 25, 1990, 85.

——— . "Familiar Line From Women Hard To Take." *The Sunday Mail*, March 10, 1991, 65.

Smith, W. "Where Do Boys Go When The Girls Go Out To Play?" *The Courier-Mail*, May 27, 1991, 29.

The Sydney Morning Herald. "Full Equality? Sorry, Madam, Not For Another 1, 000 Years." February 6, 1993, 1.

The Australian. "UN Team Urges Campaign To Lift Women's Status." August 18, 1995, 1, 4.

The Weekend Australian. "Job Equality 475 Years Off: ILO," August 26–27, 1995, 16.

Warneminde, M. "Hopes On The Ropes." *The Bulletin*, April 30, 1991, 30.

————. "A Bumper Season." *The Bulletin*, March 12, 1991, 14.

Wells, J. "Women Out Of Their League." *The Sydney Morning Herald*, August 5, 1995, 53.

————. "Propaganda Sniping At The Heritage Of Motherhood." *The Weekend Australian*, April 20–21, 1991, 30.

————. "Why Can't They Give Us A Sporting Chance For Once?" *The Australian*, June 6, 1990, 34.

————. "Beware Of Rucking With All Blondes, Simon." *The Weekend Australian*, July 21–22, 1990, 35.

————. "Dare We Risk God's Wrath Over Sheilas?" *The Australian*, August 7, 1989, 30.

————. "During The Drought Our Men Did OK." *The Australian*, August 9, 1989, 30.

————. ". . . Or Are You Just Happy To See Me?" *The Australian*, December 11, 1989, 24.

Wenzel, L. "Crying Rape!" *New Directions for Women*, May–June 1993, 4.

Subject Index

affirmative action, 4, 15, 22, 43,
    44, 46, 150, 157
  discourses of, 39–41
  hard and soft versions of,
    100, 114–15, 145
  incorporation of, xiv, 155–57
  limits of, 144–45
  managers' perceptions of, 32,
    79, 88, 97–115
  media representations of,
    117–127, 134–38
  the state and, 23–41, 129–40
antifeminism, 5, 28, 39, 88–89,
    99, 126–27
Australian Sports Commission,
    xiv, xvii, 37–39, 41, 50,
    129–138, 140–41, 148

Canadian Association for the
    Advancement of Women and
    Sport, xiv, 32, 47, 155–56
cathexis, xv, 14, 18, 19, 20, 23,
    89–94, 95, 157
childcare, xvi, 43, 57–60, 61, 95,
    133, 134, 135, 146
corporate-managerialism, xiv,
    xv, 25–46
  the state and, 25–46
cultural policy, 129, 138–140

defeminization, 86, 95
drinking behavior, 53, 56–57,
    59, 66, 81, 94

equal opportunity, 16, 25, 26,
    29, 36, 72, 89, 90, 97, 116
equity, 2, 27, 29, 33, 39–41, 67,
    70, 77, 86, 100, 102, 107, 108,
    109, 110, 112, 115, 119, 122,
    124, 126, 136, 140, 148

female managers
  barriers to, 2–3, 4, 15–16, 28,
    41–42, 48–95
  underrepresentation of, xv,
    15–16, 21, 158
feminism, 39–41, 85–89, 105,
    115, 155–57
femininity, 14, 17, 18, 85
femocrats, 27, 155

gays, 3, 17, 91–92, 94, 118, 121,
    148, 150
gender inequalities, 4–5, 7–8,
    10, 13, 18, 21–23
gender order, 14, 127, 158
gender regime, 14, 20, 23
gender stereotypes, 15, 50, 51,
    78, 83–85, 92, 117–18

glass ceiling, 15, 44, 51, 64, 66, 94, 145
groupthink, 8, 119–27, 149

heterosexism, 90, 117–118, 127, 139, 144, 150, 155
heterosexuality, 10, 13, 17, 18, 20, 41, 72, 89, 93–94
Hillary Commission for Sport, Fitness and Leisure, xiv, 33–37, 47, 157
homophobia, 3, 13, 39–40, 43, 93, 95, 111, 125, 148, 150, 152, 153
homosexuality, 90, 91, 95

individualism 28, 42, 46, 73

joking behavior, 71–72
justice, xiv, 7, 11, 27, 109, 114, 115, 130

labor, xv, 13, 14–16, 18, 20, 21, 23, 44, 51–70, 94–95, 157
lesbianism, 39, 41, 43, 86–88, 90–93, 95, 116, 121, 156

management
core and peripheral areas of, 21–22
confidence and, 75–76
men's and women's styles of, 73–79, 95
masculinity, 3, 5, 10, 13, 14, 17, 18, 20, 21, 27, 28, 42, 46, 64, 73–77, 115, 121–32, 157, 158
organizations and, 13–14, 64, 79, 107, 145–46
sport and, 19–23, 156

media, 23, 30, 39, 40, 43, 117–127, 134–36, 137–38
men, strategies for changing, 146–48
misogyny, 3, 17, 39, 40, 122, 125, 148

networks, 53–57, 67–69, 84

organizations
archetypal, 45
culture and, 11, 13, 47, 144
feminist types of, 145–46, 155–56
gender and, 13–14, 22–23, 40–46, 65–66, 74–75
intransitive types of, 64
men's resistance to women in, 97, 119, 146
proactive types of, 113–14, 149
segregation of men and women in, 13–14, 15–16, 21–22, 65–66
strategies for changing, 145–46
transitive types of, 64

power, xv, 9–11, 14, 16–18, 20–23, 39, 70–89, 92, 94, 95, 117–19, 146, 147, 157, 158
profeminism, xii, xiv, 3–11, 141, 148–53, 158

rape, 4, 6, 8, 120, 125, 148–49
reverse discrimination, 40, 101, 111, 145

sexual assault 3, 6, 8, 9, 16, 148–49

sexual discrimination, 49, 50, 61, 69, 80–81, 87, 122

sexual harassment, 4, 6, 8, 13, 16, 44, 70–72, 95, 117, 120, 148–53

sexual prejudice, 49, 50, 61, 122

sexuality, 72, 74–75, 89–95, 148

social constructionism, xiv, 3, 11, 14–23, 157

sport, strategies for changing, 148–53

Sport Canada, xiv, 30–33, 47, 156

tokenism, 2, 40, 106, 111, 115, 145

violence, 3, 16, 17, 100, 149
    sexual, 4, 6, 8–9, 16, 17, 148–51

Name Index

Abercrombie, N., 25
Acker, J., 50
Acosta, V., 143, 154
Albo, G., 25
Allan, J., 16
Allen, J., 154
Ang, I., 10
Antal, A., 15
Armstrong, N., 28
Atkinson, S., 11

Bacchi, C., 146, 158
Bagwell, S., 2
Baird, K., 117
Bentley, D., 125
Bell, E., 148
Bell, M., 36, 37, 42
Bell, S., 26
Bellamy, P., 15, 130
Bennett, J., 21
Bennett, R., 155
Bennett, T., 129, 138, 139
Bennis, W., 64
Berrett, T., 25
Birrell, S., 155, 157
Bloor, M., 50
Bluckert, P., 148
Blue, A., 121

Blum, L., 144
Bond, A., 44
Booth, A., 12
Boston, J., 25
Boyle, M., 20, 21, 23
Brackenridge, C., 48, 49
Bradshaw, J., 5
Bredemeier, B., 157
Bristow, J., 5
Brittan, A., 3
Brod, H., 3
Brown, W., 28
Bryson, L., 141
Burroughs, A., 119
Burt, S., 27, 28
Burton, C., 145

Cameron, J., 21, 22, 130
Carpenter, L., 143, 154
Casey, R., 122
Castles, F., 29
Chase, S., 83, 85
Clatterbaugh, K., 6
Coakley, J., 8
Cockburn, C., 97, 144, 145, 146,
    148, 158
Cohn C., 154
Cole, C., 157

Collins, C., 23, 34
Collinson, D., 28, 48, 64, 73, 147
Connell, R. W., 3, 4, 5, 14, 17,
    18, 19, 20, 29, 73, 127, 156
Cooper, C., 15, 97
Coser, L., 64
Couchman, P., 122, 123
Court, G., 73
Crompton, R., 50
Crossett, T., 8
Cunningham, S., 129
Curry, T., 8
Curry-Kenny, L., 43

Davidson, M., 15, 97
Davis, L., 21
Davis, N., 6
De Vrye, C., 42
Disch, L., 8
Douglas, P., 6
Dowse, S., 155
Duelli Klein, R., 5
du Gay, P., 25
Dunk, T., 157
Du Plessis, R., 25, 27, 28
Durham, M., 130

Eberhard, W., 117
Ebert, T., 19
Edgar, D., 94
Eisenstein, H., 155
Ellicott, J., 12
Elliott, H., 38, 46
Else, A., 27, 146
Epstein, C., 50

Fagenson, E., 15
Farrell, S. A., 14
Fasting, K., 49
Ferguson, J., 132, 133, 134, 140

Foley, J., 157
Franklin, S., 19
Franzway, S., 155
Freeman, S., 49
Fritner, M. P., 8
Frost, G. M., 12

Game, A., 50
Gatens, M., 148
Gaines J., 8
Gibson, J. W., 127
Gidlow, B., 34
Goode, W., 146, 147
Gordon, S., 121
Grant, J., 130
Griffin, P., 155
Gruneau, R., 21

Hall, E., 49
Hall, M. A., 7, 21, 25, 32, 48, 49,
    97, 155, 156, 157
Hall, S., 19
Harvey, J., 30
Hayes, L., 36, 37, 42
Head, B., 33
Hearn, J., 28, 50, 64, 73, 147, 148
Heath, S., 5
Heikes, E., 50
Herdt, G., 14
Hester, M., 5
Heylen Research Centre, 35
Hewitson, G., 146
Hindson, A., 25
Hinings, B., 30
Hobson, B., 132, 134, 140
Holloway, W., 157
Hood, C., 25
hooks, b., 10, 148
Hooks, D., 122
Huber, D., 20

Hughes, R., 8
Hyman, P., 27, 146

Iannello, K., 145
Izraeli, D., 15

Jackson, S., 19
James, B., 15
Jansen S., 117
Jeffords, S., 127
Johnson, A., 27
Johnson, B., 32
Johnson, C., 31

Kandiyoti, D., 14
Kane, M. J., 8, 157
Kanter, R., 73
Karpin, D., 15, 28, 130
Katz, J., 8, 148
Kavanagh, L., 120
Keat, R., 25
Keating, P., 1
Kelly, R., 41, 132, 140
Kelsey, J., 25
Kenway, J., 30, 154, 158
Kerfoot, D., 28, 73
Kidd, B., 31
Kikulius, L., 45
Kimmel, M., 3, 6, 10
Klein, A., 157
Knights, D., 28, 73
Knoppers, A., 49, 143
Koss, M., 8
Krenske, L., 157

Larner, W., 25
LaRossa, R., 61
Lavarch, M., 131
Le Feuvre, N., 50
Legge, K., 50

Lenskyj, H., 8, 9, 149, 153, 155
Liff, S., 15
Lorber, J., 14
Lorde, A., 154
Lupiano, D., 143
Lynch, L., 155

Macdonald, J., 123
Macintosh, D., 32, 33, 49
MacKinnon, C., 155
Magnay, J., 119
Maier, M., 145
Malone, P., 120
Maloney, L., 42
Mandle, B., 120
Marshall, J., 50
Martin, L., 148
Martin, P., 145, 146
Masters, R., 122, 123, 134, 135, 136, 137, 140
McBride, J., 127
McBride, S., 25
McDowell, L., 73
McGregor, J., 16
McKay, J., 20, 21, 23, 25, 117, 125, 127, 138, 139
McKeganey, N., 50
Melnick, M., 8
Messner, M., xiii, 3, 4, 5, 8, 21, 127, 148, 150
Middlemiss, I., 21, 117
Miller, P., 25
Miranda, C., 137
Myers, M., 117
Moore, M., 12
Morgan, D., 48, 50, 75
Morgan, G., 44, 68
Morrison, A., 48, 60
Morse, M., 118
Mouzelis, N., 19

215

Nauright, J., 21

Ogilvie, E., 127
Overall, C., 158

Padavic, I., 50
Parkin, W., 46, 68
Pateman, C., 30, 139
Pemberton, G., 11
Perkins, H., 34
Pfiel, F., 127
Phillips, D., 120
Phillips, J., 157
Poidevin, S., 121
Poiner, G., 144
Porter, P., 130
Powell, G., 15, 113, 131
Pringle, R., 28, 39, 49, 50
Pronger, B., 157
Punch, G., 37
Pusey, M., 26, 30

Radford Ruether, R., 6–7
Raivio, M. R., 49
Ramsay, K., 15, 130
Rees, S., 25
Reskin, B., 48, 66, 97
Richardson, D., 5
Richter, D., 155
Robert, E., 28, 64, 73
Robinson, V., 5
Roos, P., 48, 66, 97
Roper, M., 49, 50, 64, 73
Rose, N., 25
Rowe, D., 118
Rubinson, L., 8
Ruth, S., 148

Sabo, D., 8, 117, 148, 150
Samaranch, J. A., 1

Sanday, P., 14
Saville-Smith, K., 15
Sawer, M., 28
Schein, V., 2
Scutt, J., 43
Semotiuk, D., 30
Shaver, S., 158
Shields, J., 25
Simmons, M., 148
Sinclair, A., 98
Sisjord, M. K., 49
Slack, T., 30
Smart, G., 120, 124
Smith, P., 21
Smith, V., 144
Smith, W., 124
Smith, Y., 157
Spender, D., 141
Stanley, L., 5
Starhawk, 11
Steinberg, R., 155
Still, L., 15
Stolcke, V., 154
Stuart, M., 23, 34

Tanton, M., 15
Taylor, R., 8
Theberge, N., 155
Thompson, S., 21, 138
Thornton, M., 144
Timpson, M., 130
Trujillo, N., 19, 118, 157

Vilkinas, T., 15
Volkerling, J., 34

Wajcman, J., 15
Walby, S., 19
Wark, M., 129
Warneminde, M., 123, 124

Watson, S., 28, 39, 155
Weeks, J., 14, 148
Wells, J., 119, 120, 121, 124
Wenzel, L., 9
West, A., 49
West, Candice, 19
West, Cornel, 14
White, A., 48, 49
White, G., 8
Whitson, D., 21, 32, 33, 49
Wieneke, C., 27, 130, 144
Williams, C., 49, 50
Williams, J., 8

Willmott, H., 25
Wills, S., 144
Winter, M., 28, 64, 73
Wise, S., 5
Witz, A., 158
Woldring, K., 15

Yeatman, A., 25, 27, 28, 30, 146, 155
Young, I., 148

Zimmerman, D., 14